INSIGHT GUIDES

KU-033-809

DANISH

PHRASEBOOK & DICTIONARY

Contacting the Editors

Every effort has been made to provide accurate information in this publication, but changes are inevitable. The publisher cannot be responsible for any resulting loss, inconvenience or injury. We would appreciate it if readers would call our attention to any errors or outdated information. We also welcome your suggestions; if you come across a relevant expression not in our phrase book, please contact us at: hello@insightguides.com

All Rights Reserved
2016 Apa Digital (CH) AG and Apa Publications (UK) Ltd.

First Edition: 2016
Printed in China

Cover & Interior Design: Pawel Pasternak
Production: AM Services
Production Manager: Vicky Glover
Cover Photo: Shutterstock

Interior Photos: Shutterstock

CONTENTS

ACTIVITIES

HEALTH & SAFETY

PRONUNCIATION

This section is designed to make you familiar with the sounds of Danish by using our simplified phonetic transcription. You'll find the pronunciation of the Danish letters and sounds explained below, together with their 'imitated' equivalents. This system is used throughout the phrase book: simply read the pronunciation as if it were English, noting any special rules below.

Stress has been indicated in the phonetic transcription with underlining. Bold on vowels indicates a lengthening of the vowel sound.

CONSONANTS

Letter	Approximate Pronunciation	Symbol	Example	Pronunciation
c	1. before e, i, y, like s in sit	**s**	**citron**	*see • troan*
	2. before a, o, u and K a consonant, like k in kite	**k**	**cafeteria**	*kah • feh • teh • ree • a*
d	1. at the end of the word after a vowel, or between a vowel and unstressed e or i, like th in this[1]	**dh**	**med**	*medh*
	2. otherwise, as in English	**d**	**dale**	*da • ler*

[1] The letter **d** is not pronounced in **nd** and **ld** at the end of a word or syllable (**guld** = gooll), or before unstressed **e**, **t** or **s** in the same syllable (**plads** = plass).

Letter	Approximate Pronunciation	Symbol	Example	Pronunciation
g	1. at the beginning of a word or syllable, like g in go	g	glas	*glas*
	2. otherwise, like y in yet[2]	y	sige	*see • yer*
hv	like v in view	v	hvor	*voar*
j, hj	like y in yet	y	ja	*ya*
k	1. between vowels, like g in go	g	ikke	*ig • ger*
	2. otherwise like k in kite	k	kaffe	*kah • fer*
ng	like ng in sing	ng	ingen	*ing • ern*
p	1. between vowels, like b in bit	b	stoppe	*stoh • ber*
	2. otherwise like p in pill	p	pude	*poo • dher*
r	at the beginning of a word, pronounced in the back of the throat, but otherwise often omitted	r	rose	*roa • ser*
s	like s in see	s	skål	*skowl*

[2] The letter **g** occasionally sounds like **ch** in Scottish loch and can sometimes be mute after **a**, **e**, **o**.

Letter	Approximate Pronunciation	Symbol	Example	Pronunciation
sj	usually like sh in sheet	sh	sjælden	*sheh • lern*

t	1. between vowels, like d in do	d	lytte	_lew_ • der
	2. otherwise like t in to	t	torsk	toarsk

Letters b, f, h, l, m, n, v are generally pronounced as in English.

VOWELS

Letter	Approximate Pronunciation	Symbol	Example	Pronunciation
a	1. when long, like a in father	ah	klare	_klah_ • rah
	2. when short, like a in cat	a	hat	hat
e	1. when long, like er in fern	er	svare	_svah_ • rer
	2. when short, like e in met	eh	let	leht
i	1. when long, like ee in bee	ee	ile	_ee_ • ler
	2. when short, like i in pin[3]	i	drikke	drig • ger

[3] In nouns that end with an **e**, an **r** is added to create the plural. In verbs that end with an **e**, an **r** at the end indicates the first person form. This **er** sound, in both cases, sounds like **ah**.

SOUND COMBINATIONS

Letter	Approximate Pronunciation	Symbol	Example	Pronunciation
o	1. when long, like oa in boat	oa	sol	_soal_
	2. when short, like o in lot	oh	godt	_goht_
u	1. when long, oo in pool	oo	frue	_froo • er_
	2. when short, like oa in boat	oa	luft	_loaft_
y	like ew in new	ew	nyde	_new • dher_
æ	1. when long, like ay in day	ay	sæbe	_say • ber_
	2. when short, like e in get	eh	ægte	_ehg • ter_
ø	like ur in fur	ur	frøken	_frur • kern_
å	1. when long, like ow in tow	ow	åben	_ow • bern_
	2. when short, like aw in saw	aw	sådan	_saw • dan_

ⓘ

A vowel is generally long in stressed syllables when it's the final letter or followed by only one consonant. If followed by two or more consonants, or in unstressed syllables, the vowel is generally short.

In or after some vowels, a short puff of air (glottal stop) is added following the sound. The glottal stop significantly changes the meaning of certain words, e.g., tænder with a glottal stop means 'teeth', whereas tænder without a glottal stop means 'to turn on'. As foreigners will be understood without using the glottal stop, this sound has not been included in the phonetics.

VOWELS

Letter	Approximate Pronunciation	Symbol	Example	Pronunciation
av, af	like	**ow**	**hav**	*how*
ej, eg	like ie in lie	**ie**	**nej**	*nie*
ev	like e in get plus oo sound	**eu**	**levned**	*leu • nerdh*
ov	like ow in show	**ow**	**sjov**	*show*
øj	ike oi in oil	**oi**	**øje**	*oi • er*
øv	like o in so	**oh**	**søvnig**	*soh • nee*

Dansk (Danish), a North Germanic language related to Norwegian, Swedish and Icelandic, is the official language of Denmark.
There are about six million native speakers in Denmark and parts of northern Germany.
Danish is an official language of the autonomous territories of Greenland and the Faroe Islands, in addition to Greenlandic and Farocse.

HOW TO USE THE APP

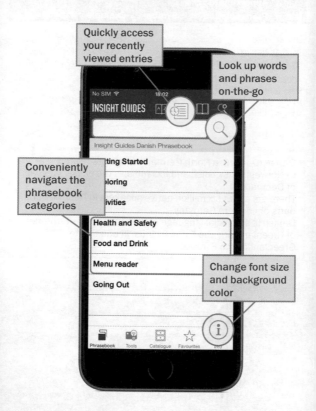

Quickly access your recently viewed entries

Look up words and phrases on-the-go

Conveniently navigate the phrasebook categories

Change font size and background color

Save the most useful everyday words and phrases to your Favorites

Use the Flash Cards Quiz to learn and memorize new words easily

Take all digital advantages of the app: listen to words and phrases pronounced by native speakers

To learn how to activate the app, see the inside back cover of this phrasebook.

GRAMMAR

REGULAR VERBS

The present tense of regular verbs in Danish is formed by adding **-r** to the infinitive. The past tense is formed by adding **-de** to the infinitive or **-te** to the root. The future is formed by using the present tense of **ville** (will) + the verb in the infinitive. This applies to all persons (e.g., I, you, he, she, it, etc.). Following are the present, past and future forms of the verbs **at snakke** (to speak) and **at spise** (to eat). The different conjugation endings are in bold.

for. =formal   inf. = informal
sing. = singular   pl. = plural

	PRESENT	PAST	FUTURE
at snakke (to speak)	snakk**er**	snakke**de**	vil snakke
at spise (to eat)	spis**er**	**spiste**	**vil spise**

PRONOUNS	
I	**jeg**
you (sing. inf./for.)	**du/De**
he	**han**
she	**hun**
it (common/neuter)	**den/det**
we	**vi**
you (pl.)	**I**
they	**de**

IRREGULAR VERBS

There are a number of irregular verbs in Danish; these must be memorized. Like regular verbs, however, the irregular verb form remains the same, irrespective of person. Following are the present, past and future conjugations for a number of important, useful irregular verbs.

	PRESENT	PAST	FUTURE
at være (to be)	er	var	vil være
at have (to have)	har	havde	vil have
at kunne (to be able)	kan	kunne	vil kunne
at gå (to walk)	går	gik	vil gå
at tage (to take)	tager	tog	vil tage

WORD ORDER

Danish is similar to English in terms of word order for simple sentences: It follows the subject-verb-object pattern.

Example: **Vi efterlader vores bagage her.** We leave our luggage here.

When the sentence doesn't begin with a subject, the word order changes; the verb and the subject are inverted.

Questions are formed by reversing the order of the subject and verb:

Du ser bilen.	You see the car.
Ser du bilen?	Do you see the car?

NEGATION

A statement can be negated by inserting the word **ikke** after the verb:

Jeg taler dansk.	I speak Danish.
Jeg taler ikke dansk.	I do not speak Danish.

IMPERATIVES

The imperative is exactly the same form as the stem of the verb:

Rejs!	Travel!	**Gå!**	Walk!
Tro!	Believe!	**Spis!**	Eat!

NOUNS & ARTICLES

The indefinite article (a, an) is expressed with **en** for common nouns and with **et** for neuter nouns. Generally, common nouns are those that can be both feminine and masculine (e.g. people, animals, etc.); neuter nouns have no gender (e.g. house, roof, etc.). However, note that there are several exceptions to this rule. Indefinite plurals are formed by adding **-e, -r** or **-er** to the singular.

PRONOUNS				
common	**en pige**	a girl	**piger**	girls
neuter	**et hus**	a house	**huse**	houses

Some nouns remain unchanged in the plural, for example:

et rum	a room
rum	rooms

Definite articles: Where in English we say 'the car', the Danes say the equivalent of 'car-the', i.e. they tag the definite article onto the end of the noun. In the singular, common nouns take an **-en** ending, neuter nouns an **-et** ending. In the plural, both take an **-(e)ne** or **-(er)ne** ending.

	SINGULAR		PLURAL	
common	**kanin**	the rabbit	**kaninerne**	the rabbits
neuter	**toget**	the train	**togene**	the trains

ADJECTIVES

Adjectives usually precede nouns. In certain circumstances, the adjective takes an ending. In the singular indefinite form, adjectives remain unchanged but, in the plural indefinite form, with both common and neuter nouns, the adjective takes an -e ending.

	SINGULAR		PLURAL	
common	en stor bil	a big car	store biler	big cars
neuter	et stort hus	a big house	store huse	big houses

In the definite form, an adjective takes an -e ending with both common and neuter nouns, in both the singular and plural. However, in this definite usage, **den** must be placed in front of the adjective in the case of common nouns in the singular, **det** in the case of singular neuter nouns and **de** with any plural.

	SINGULAR		PLURAL	
common	**den** store bil	the big car	**de** stor e biler	the big cars
neuter	**det** store hus	the big house	**de** store huse	the big houses

ADVERBS AND ADVERBIAL EXPRESSIONS

Adverbs are generally formed by adding -t to the corresponding adjective.

Hun går hurtigt.	She walks quickly.
Hun går en hurtig tur.	She has a quick walk.

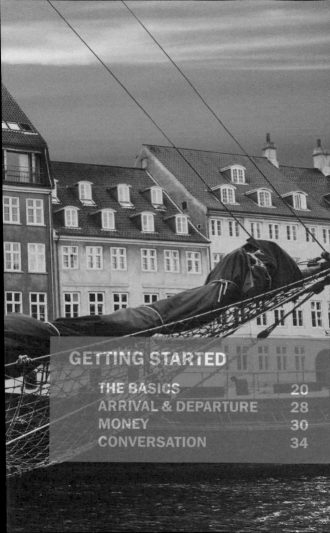

GETTING STARTED

THE BASICS

NUMBERS

NEED TO KNOW

0	**nul**
	noal
1	**en**
	ehn
2	**to**
	toa
3	**tre**
	treh
4	**fire**
	fee•ah
5	**fem**
	fehm
6	**seks**
	sehks
7	**syv**
	sew
8	**otte**
	<u>oa</u>•der
9	**ni**
	nee
10	**ti**
	tee
11	**elleve**
	<u>ehl</u>•ver
12	**tolv**
	toal

13	**tretten**	
	treh • dern	
14	**fjorten**	
	fyoar • dern	
15	**femten**	
	fehm • dern	
16	**seksten**	
	sie • stern	
17	**sytten**	
	sur • dern	
18	**atten**	
	a • dern	
19	**nitten**	
	ni • dern	
20	**tyve**	
	tew • ver	
21	**enogtyve**	
	ehn • oh • tew • ver	
22	**tooggyve**	
	toa • oh • tew • ver	
30	**tredive**	
	trehdh • ver	
31	**enogtredive**	
	ehn • oh • trehdh • ver	
40	**fyrre**	
	fur • er	
50	**halvtreds**	
	hal • trehs	
60	**tres**	
	trehs	
70	**halvfjerds**	
	hal • fyehrs	
80	**firs**	
	feers	

90	**halvfems**
	hal • fehms
100	**hundrede**
	hoon • rah • dher
101	**hundrede og et**
	hoon • rah • dher ow eht
200	**to hundrede**
	toa hoon • rah • dher
500	**fem hundrede**
	fehm hoon • rah • dher
1000	**tusind**
	too • sin
10,000	**ti tusind**
	tee too • sin
1,000,000	**en million**
	ehn meel • yoan

ORDINAL NUMBERS

first	**første**
	furs • der
second	**anden/andet**
	an • ern/an • erdh
third	**tredje**
	trehdh • yer
fourth	**fjerde**
	fyay • ah
fifth	**femte**
	fehm • der
once	**en gang**
	ehn gahng
twice	**to gange**
	toa gahng • er
three times	**tre gange**
	treh gahng • er

TIME

NEED TO KNOW

What time is it?	**Hvad er klokken?**
	vadh ehr kloh • gern
It's noon [midday].	**Klokken er tolv.**
	kloh • gern ehr tohl
At midnight.	**Ved midnat.**
	vedh meedh • nat
From nine o'clock to five o'clock.	**Fra klokken ni til sytten.**
	frah kloh • gern nee til surd • den
Twenty after [past] four.	**Tyve minutter over fire.**
	tew • ver mee • noo • dah ow • ah fee • ah
A quarter to nine.	**Kvart i ni.**
	kvaht ee nee
5:30 a.m./p.m.	**Halv seks om morgenen/aftenen.**
	hal sehks ohm moh • nern/af • tern

DAYS

NEED TO KNOW

Monday	**mandag**
	man • da
Tuesday	**tirsdag**
	teers • da
Wednesday	**onsdag**
	oans • da
Thursday	**torsdag**
	tohs • da
Friday	**fredag**
	freh • da
Saturday	**lørdag**
	lur • da
Sunday	**søndag**
	surn • da

DATES

yesterday	**i går**
	ee _gaw_
today	**i dag**
	ee da
tomorrow	**i morgen**
	ee mohn
day	**dag**
	da
week	**uge**
	_oo_ • er
month	**måned**
	mow • nerdh

year	**år**
	aw

Denmark follows a day-month-year format instead of the month-day-year format used in the U.S.
E.g.: July 25, 2008; 25/07/08 = 7/25/2008 in the U.S.

MONTHS

January	**januar**
	ya • noo • ah
February	**februar**
	feh • broo • ah
March	**marts**
	mahts
April	**april**
	a • preel
May	**maj**
	mie
June	**juni**
	yoo • nee

July	**juli**
	yoo • lee
August	**august**
	ow • goast
September	**september**
	sehp • tehm • bah
October	**oktober**
	ohk • toa • bah
November	**november**
	noa • vehm • bah
December	**december**
	deh • sehm • bah

SEASONS

spring	**forår**
	foh • aw
summer	**sommer**
	sohm • mah
fall [autumn]	**efterår**
	ehf • dah • aw
winter	**vinter**
	vin • dah

HOLIDAYS

January 1, New Year's Day	**Nytårsdag**
June 5, Constitution Day (afternoon only)	**Grundlovsdag**
December 24, Christmas Eve	**Juleaften**
December 25, Christmas Day	**Første juledag**
December 26, Boxing Day	**Anden juledag**
Maundy Thursday	**Skærtorsdag**
Good Friday	**Langfredag**
Easter Sunday	**Første påskedag**
Easter Monday	**Anden påskedag**
General Prayer Day	**Store Bededag**
Ascension Day	**Kristi himmelfart**

ARRIVAL & DEPARTURE

NEED TO KNOW

I'm here on vacation [holiday]/business.

Jeger her på ferie/forretningsrejse.
yie ehr hehr paw <u>fehr</u> • yer/ foh • <u>reht</u> • nings • rie • ser

I'm going to…

Jeg skal til…
yie skal til…

I'm staying at the …Hotel.

Jeg bor på Hotel…
yie boar paw hoa • <u>tehl</u>…

YOU MAY HEAR…

Din billet/Dit pas, tak.
deen <u>bee</u> • lehd/deet pas tahk

Hvad er formålet med din rejse?
vadh ehr <u>foh</u> • mow • lehdh medh deen <u>rie</u> • ser

Hvor skal du bo?
voar skal doo boa

Your ticket/ passport, please.

What's the purpose of your visit?

Where are you staying?

Hvor lang tid skal du være her?
voar langh teedh skal doo <u>vay</u> • er hehr

Hvem rejser du sammen med?
vehm <u>rie</u> • ser doo <u>sahm</u> • ern medh

How long are you staying?
Who are you with?

BORDER CONTROL

YOU MAY HEAR...

Har du noget at fortolde?
har doo <u>noa</u> • erdh ad for • <u>toh</u> • ler

Du skal betale told af det her.
doo skal beh • <u>ta</u> • ler tohl a deh hehr

Vær venlig at åbne denne taske.
vehr <u>vehn</u> • lee ad <u>owb</u> • ner <u>deh</u> • ner <u>tas</u> • ger

Do you have anything to declare?
You must pay duty on this.
Please open this bag.

I'm just passing through.	**Jeg er her kun på gennemrejse.**
	yie ehr hehr koon paw <u>geh</u>•nehm•rie•ser
I would like to declare...	**Jeg vil gerne fortolde...**
	yie vil <u>gehr</u>•ner for•<u>toh</u>•ler...
I have nothing to declare.	**Jeg har ikke noget at fortolde.**
	yie hah <u>ig</u>•ger <u>noa</u>•erdh ad foh•<u>toh</u>•ler

YOU MAY SEE...

TOLD	customs
TOLDFRIE VARER	duty-free goods
VARER AT ANGIVE	goods to declare
INGEN VARER AT ANGIVE	nothing to declare
TOLDFRIT	duty-free
PASKONTROL	passport control
POLITI	police

MONEY

Where's...?	**Hvor er...?**
	voar ehr...
the ATM	**pengeautomaten**
	<u>pehng</u>•er•ow•toa•ma•dern
the bank	**banken**
	<u>bahnk</u>•ern
the currency exchange office	**vekselkontor**
	<u>vehk</u>•serl•kohn•toar
What time does the bank open/close?	**Hvornår åbner/lukker banken?**
	voar•<u>naw owb</u>•nah/<u>loa</u>•gah <u>bahnk</u>•ern

I'd like to change dollars/pounds into kroner.	**Jeg vil gerne veksle nogle dollars/pund til kroner.** *yie vil <u>gehr</u>•ner <u>vehks</u>•ler noa•ler <u>doh</u>•lahs/poon til <u>kroa</u>•ner*
I want to cash a traveler's check [cheque].	**Jeg vil gerne indløse en rejsecheck.** *yie vil <u>gehr</u>•ner <u>in</u>•lur•ser ehn <u>rie</u>•ser•shehk*

AT THE BANK

Can I exchange foreign currency here?	**Kan jeg veksle penge her?** *kan yie <u>vehk</u>•sler <u>pehng</u>•er hehr*
What's the exchange rate?	**Hvad er vekselkursen?** *vadh ehr <u>vehk</u>•serl•koor•sern*
I think there's a mistake.	**Jeg tror der er begået en fejl.** *yie troar dehr ehr be•gow•erd ehn fiel*
How much is the fee?	**Hvor meget beregner du i kommission?** *voar <u>mie</u>•erdh beh•<u>rie</u>•ner doo ee koa•mee•<u>shoan</u>*

I've lost my traveler's checks [cheques].	**Jeg har tabt mine rejsechecks.** *yie hah tahbd mee•ner rie•ser•shehks*
My card was lost.	**Jeg har tabt mit kort.** *yie hah tahbd meed kawd*
My credit cards were stolen.	**Mine kort er blevet stjålet.** *mee•ner kawd ehr bleh•verdh stjow•lerd*
My card doesn't work.	**Mit kort virker ikke.** *meed kawd veer•gah ig•ger*
The ATM ate my card.	**Pengeautomaten tog mit kort.** *Pehng•er•ow•toa•ma•dern toh meet kawd*

For Numbers, see page 20.

(i)

Cash can be obtained from **pengeautomater** (ATMs), which are located throughout Denmark. Some debit cards (with the Plusand Cirrus logos) and most major credit cards are accepted. Be sure you know your PIN and whether it is compatible with European machines, which usually expect a four-digit, numeric code. ATMs offer good rates, though there may be some hidden fees.

Vekselkontor (currency exchange offices) and **banker** (banks) are options for exchanging currency. Exchange offices are found in many tourist centers. Banks in Copenhagen are open Monday to Friday 9:30 a.m. to 4:00 p.m., with some branches open late on Thursdays. Currency exchange offices and banks charge similar fees to exchange money. Remember to bring your passport for identification.

YOU MAY SEE...

INDSÆT DIT KORT	insert card
ANNULLER	cancel
SLET	clear
INDTAST	enter
PINKODE	PIN
UDBETALING	withdraw funds
FRA DIN CHECKKONTO	from checking [current] account
FRA DIN OPSPARINGSKONTO	from savings account
KVITTERING	receipt

Denmark, Norway and Sweden all use the same name for their currency, but the value differs in each country. The **krone** (meaning 'crown', pronounced _kroa_ • ner and abbreviated **kr.** or **DKK**), is divided into 100 øre (pronounced _ur_ • er).
Coins: 25 and 50 **øre**, 1, 2, 5, 10 and 20 **kroner**
Notes: 50, 100, 200, 500 and 1,000 **kroner**

CONVERSATION

NEED TO KNOW

Hello!	**Hej!**
	hie
How are you?	**Hvordan har du det?**
	voar•<u>dan</u> har doo deh
Fine, thanks.	**Godt, tak.**
	goht tahk
Excuse me!	**Undskyld!**
	<u>oan</u>•skewl
Do you speak	**Kan du tale engelsk?**
English?	*kan doo <u>ta</u>•ler ehng•erlsk*
What's your name?	**Hvad hedder du?**
	vadh <u>heh</u>•dhah doo
My name is...	**Mit navn er...**
	meet nown ehr...
Nice to meet you.	**Det glæder mig at træffe dig.**
	deh <u>glay</u>•dhah mie ad <u>treh</u>•fer die
Where are you from?	**Hvor kommer du fra?**
	voar <u>koh</u>•mah doo frah
I'm from the U.S./	**Jeg kommer fra USA/England.**
the U.K.	*yie <u>koh</u>•mah frah oo•ehs•a/*
	ehng•lan
What do you do?	**Hvad laver du?**
	vadh <u>la</u>•vah doo
I work for...	**Jeg arbejder hos...**
	yie <u>ah</u>•bey•dah hohs...
I'm a student.	**Jeg studerer.**
	yie stoo•<u>deh</u>•rah
I'm retired.	**Jeg er pensionist.**
	yie ehr pang•shoa•<u>neest</u>

Do you like...?	**Kan du lide...?**
	kan doo lee...
Goodbye.	**Farvel.**
	fah • vehl
See you later.	**På gensyn.**
	paw gehn • sewn

LANGUAGE DIFFICULTIES

Do you speak English?	**Kan du tale engelsk?**
	kan doo ta • ler ehng • erlsk
Does anyone here speak English?	**Er der nogen her, der kan tale engelsk?**
	ehr dehr noa • ern hehr dehr kan ta • ler ehng • erlsk
I don't speak (much) Danish.	**Jeg kan ikke tale (ret meget) dansk.**
	yie kan ig • ger ta • ler (reht mie • erdh) dansk
Can you speak more slowly?	**Kan du tale lidt langsommere?**
	kan doo ta • ler lit lang • sohm • ah
Can you repeat that?	**Kan du gentage det?**
	kan doo gehn • ta • yer deh
What was that?	**Hvad var det?**
	vadh vah deh
Can you spell it?	**Kan du stave til det?**
	kan doo stawe deh
Please write it down.	**Vær rar og skriv det ned.**
	vehr rah ow skreew deh nedh
Can you translate this for mc?	**Kan du oversætte det her for mig?**
	kan doo oh • wah • sch • der dch hchr for mie
What does this mean?	**Hvad betyder det her?**
	vadh beh • tew • dhah deh hehr

I understand.	**Jeg forstår det godt.**
	yie foh • <u>staw</u> deh goht
I don't understand.	**Jeg forstår det ikke.**
	yie foh • <u>staw</u> deh ig • ger
Do you understand?	**Kan du forstå det?**
	kan doo foh • <u>staw</u> deh

De (the formal form of *you*) is generally no longer used to address strangers, but is restricted to formal letters, addressing the elderly or addressing members of the royal family. As a general rule, **du** can be used in all situations without offending anyone.

MAKING FRIENDS

YOU MAY HEAR...

Jeg taler kun lidt engelsk.	I only speak
yie <u>ta</u> • lah koon lit <u>ehng</u> • erlsk	a little English.
Jeg kan ikke tale engelsk.	I don't speak
yie kan <u>ig</u> • ger <u>ta</u> • ler <u>ehng</u> • erlsk	English.

Hello!	**Hej!**
	hie
Good morning.	**God morgen.**
	goadh • <u>mohn</u>
Good afternoon.	**God eftermiddag.**
	goadh • <u>ef</u> • tah • mi • da
Good evening.	**God aften.**
	goadh • <u>ahf</u> • tern
My name is...	**Mit navn er...**
	meet nown ehr...

What's your name?	**Hvad hedder du?**
	vadh <u>heh</u> • dhah doo
Let me introduce	**Lad mig præsentere dig for...**
you to...	*ladh mie pray • sehn • <u>teh</u> • rer die foh...*
Nice to meet you.	**Det glæder mig at træffe dig.**
	deh <u>glay</u> • dhah mie ad <u>tray</u> • fer die
How are you?	**Hvordan har du det?**
	voar • <u>dan</u> hah doo deh
Fine, thanks.	**Godt, tak.**
	goht tahk
And you?	**Og hvordan har du det?**
	ow voar • <u>dan</u> hah doo deh

In Denmark, upon meeting, it is customary to shake hands for both men and women. Close friends (male-female/female-female) may give kisses on the cheeks. As a greeting, you could say **Går det godt?** (How's it going?) or **Hva så?** (What's up?). **Hej** is used both for *hello* or *hi* and *bye*.

TRAVEL TALK

I'm here...	**Jeg er her...**
	yie ehr hehr...
on business	**på forretningsrejse**
	pow foh • <u>reht</u> • nings • rie • ser
on vacation	**på ferie**
[holiday]	*paw <u>fehr</u> • yer*
studying	**for at studere**
	foh ad stoo • <u>deh</u> • er
I'm staying for...	**Jeg skal være her...**
	yie skal <u>vay</u> • ah hehr...
I've been here...	**Jeg har været her...**
	yie hah <u>vay</u> • erdh hehr...

a day	**en dag**
	ehn da
a week	**en uge**
	ehn oo • er
a month	**en måned**
	ehn mow • nerdh
Where are you from?	**Hvor kommer du fra?**
	voar koh • mah doo frah
I'm from…	**Jeg kommer fra…**
	yie koh • mah frah…

For Numbers, see page 20.

PERSONAL

Who are you with?	**Hvem er du her sammen med?**
	vehm ehr doo hehr sah • mern mehdh
I'm on my own.	**Jeg er her alene.**
	yie ehr hehr a • leh • ner
I'm with…	**Jeg er her sammen med…**
	yie ehr hehr sah • mern mehdh…
my husband/wife	**min mand/kone**
	meen man/koa • ner
my boyfriend/ girlfriend	**min kæreste**
	meen kehr • sder
a friend	**en ven**
	ehn vehn
a colleague	**en kollega**
	ehn koa • leh • ga
When's your birthday?	**Hvornår et det din fødselsdag?**
	voar • naw ehr deh deen fur • sehls • da
How old are you?	**Hvor gammel er du?**
	voar gah • merl ehr doo
I'm…	**Jeg er…**
	yie ehr…

Are you married?	**Er du gift?**
	ehr doo geefd
I'm...	**Jeg er...**
	yie ehr...
single	**ugift**
	<u>oo</u> • geefd
in a relationship	**i et seriøst forhold**
	ee eht seh • ree • <u>ursd</u> foh • hohl
engaged	**forlovet**
	for • lowedh
married	**gift**
	geefd
divorced	**skilt**
	skild
separated	**separeret**
	seh • pah • <u>reh</u> • erdh
I'm widowed.	**Jeg er enkemand** *m* **/enke** *f.*
	yie ehr <u>ehn</u> • ker • man/<u>ehn</u> • ker
Do you have children/ grandchildren?	**Har du nogen børn/børnebørn?**
	hah doo noa • ern burn/<u>bur</u> • ner • burn

WORK & SCHOOL

What do you do?	**Hvad laver du?**
	vadh __la__ • ver doo
What are you studying?	**Hvad studerer du?**
	vadh stoo • __deh__ • ah doo
I'm studying...	**Jeg studerer...**
	yie stoo • __deh__ • ah...
I work full time/part time.	**Jeg arbejder fuldtids/deltids.**
	yie ah • bey • dah __fool__ • teedhs/ __dehl__ • teedhs
I work at home.	**Jeg arbejder hjemmefra.**
	*yie **ah** • bey • dah __yeh__ • mer • frah*
I'm unemployed.	**Jeg er arbejdsløs**
	yie ehr arh • bieydhs • lurs
Who do you work for?	**Hvor arbejder du henne?**
	voar ah • bey • dah doo __heh__ • ner
I work for...	**Jeg arbejder hos...**
	*yie **ah** • bey • dah hohs...*
Here's my business card	**Her er mit visitkort.**
	hehr ehr meet vee • __seet__ • kawd

WEATHER

What's the weather forecast?	**Hvordan er vejrudsigten?**
	voar • __dan__ ehr __vehr__ • oodh • sig • dern
What beautiful/ terrible weather!	**Hvor er det smukt/frygteligt vejr!**
	voar ehr deh smoagt/__frurg__ • ter • leed vayr
It's...	**Det...**
	deh...
cold	**koldt**
	kohldh
cool	**er koldt**
	ehr kohlt

hot	**hot**
	hodh
icy	**er iskoldt**
	ehr <u>ees</u> • kohlt
rainy	**regner**
	<u>rie</u> • nah
snowy	**sner**
	snehr
warm	**er varmt**
	ehr vahmt
It's sunny.	**Solen skinner.**
	<u>soa</u> • lern <u>ski</u> • nah
Do I need a jacket/	**Har jeg brug for en jakke/paraply?**
an umbrella?	*hah yie broo foh ehn <u>yah</u> • ker/*
	pah • rah • <u>plew</u>

For Seasons, see page 26.

EXPLORING

GETTING AROUND

NEED TO KNOW

How do I get to town?	**Hvordan kommer jeg ind til byen?**
	voar • dan kohm • ah yie in til bew • ern
Where's...?	**Hvor er...?**
	voar ehr...
the airport	**lufthavnen**
	loaft • hown • ern
the train [railway] station	**togstationen**
	tow • sta • shoa • nern
the bus station	**busstationen**
	boos • sta • shoa • nern
the subway [underground] station	**metrostationen**
	meh • troa • sta • shoan • nern
How far is it?	**Hvor langt er der?**
	voar lahngt ehr dehr
Where can I buy tickets?	**Hvor køber man billetter?**
	voar kur • ber man bee • leh • dah
A one-way/ return ticket.	**En enkeltbillet/returbillet.**
	ehn ehn • kerld • bee • lehd/ reh • toor • bee • lehd

How much?	**Hvor meget koster det?**
	voar <u>mie</u> • erdh <u>kohs</u> • dah deh
Are there any discounts?	**Er der nogen rabatter?**
	ehr der noa • ern rah • <u>ba</u> • dah
Which...?	**Hvilken...?**
	<u>vil</u> • kern...
gate	**gate**
	gayd
line	**tog**
	tow
platform	**perron**
	peh • <u>rohng</u>
Where can I get a taxi?	**Hvor kan jeg få en taxa?**
	voar kan yie fow ehn tahk • sa
Take me to this address.	**Kør mig til denne adresse.**
	kur mie til <u>deh</u> • ner a • <u>drah</u> • ser
Where can I rent a car?	**Hvor kan jeg leje en bil?**
	voar kan yie <u>lie</u> • er ehn beel
Can I have a map?	**Har du et vejkort?**
	har doo eht <u>vie</u> • kawd

TICKETS

When's...to Århus?	**Hvornår afgår...til Århus?**
	voar • <u>naw</u> <u>ow</u> • gaw...til <u>aw</u> • hoos
the first bus	**den første bus**
	dehn <u>fur</u> • sder boos
the next flight	**det næste fly**
	deh <u>nehs</u> • der flew
the last train	**det sidste tog**
	deh <u>sees</u> • der tow

YOU MAY HEAR...

Hvilket flyselskab rejser du med?
vil • gerdh <u>flew</u> • sehl • skab <u>rie</u> • ser doo medh

What airline are you flying?

Indenrigs eller udenrigs?
in • ern • <u>rees</u> ehl • er <u>oo</u> • dhern • rees

Domestic or International?

Hvilken terminal?
vil • gern tehr • mee • <u>nal</u>

What terminal?

Where can I buy tickets?	**Hvor køber man billetter?** _voar <u>kur</u> • berman bee • <u>lehd</u> • ah_
One ticket/Two tickets, please.	**En billet/To billetter, tak.** _ehn bee • <u>lehd</u>/toa bee • <u>leh</u> • dah tahk_
For today/tomorrow.	**Til i dag/i morgen.** _til ee • <u>dah</u>/ee • <u>mawn</u>_
A (an)...ticket.	**...billet.** _...bee • <u>lehd</u>_
one-way [single]	**En enkelt** _ehn <u>ehn</u> • kerld_
return trip	**En retur** _ehn reh • <u>toor</u>_

first class	**En førsteklasse**
	ehn furs • der kla • ser
business class	**En business class**
	ehn beesh • nesh klass
economy class	**En økonomiklasse**
	ehn ur • koa • noa • mee • kla • ser
How much?	**Hvor meget?**
	voar mie • erdh
Is there a discount for...?	**Er der rabat for...?**
	ehr dehr rah • bat foh...
chIldren	**børn**
	burn
students	**studerende**
	stoo • deh • reh • ner
senior citizens	**pensionister**
	pang • shoa • nees • dah
tourists	**turister**
	tuh • rist • ehr
The express bus/ express train, please.	**Hvor er ekspresbussen/lyntoget?**
	voar ehr ehks • prehs boo • sern/ lewn • tow • erdh
The local bus/train, please.	**Hvor er lokalbussen/regionaltoget?**
	voar ehr loa • kal • boo • sern/ reh • gee • onal • tow • erdh
I have an e-ticket.	**Jeg har en e-billet.**
	yie har ehn eh • bee • lehd
Can I buy a ticket on the bus/train?	**Kan jeg købe en billet i bussen/toget?**
	kan yie kur • ber ehn bee • lehd ee boo • sern/tow • erdh
Do I have to stamp the ticket before boarding?	**Skal jeg stemple billetten, inden jeg står på?**
	skal yie stem • pler bee • lehden, in • ern yie staw pow
How long is this ticket valid?	**Hvor længe gælder billetten?**
	voar layng • er gayl • dehr bee • lehd • ern

Can I return on the same ticket?	**Kan jeg komme tilbage med samme billet?**
	kan yie kohm • ah til • ba • yer medh
	sahm • ern bee • lehd
I'd like to...my reservation.	**Jeg vil gerne...min bestilling.**
	yie vil <u>gehr</u> • ner...meen beh • <u>stil</u> • ing
cancel	**annullere**
	<u>a</u> • noo • leh • rah
change	**ændre**
	<u>ehn</u> • drer
confirm	**bekræfte**
	beh • <u>krehf</u> • der

For Days, see page 24.

AIRPORT TRANSFER

How much is a taxi to the airport?	**Hvor meget koster en taxa til lufthavnen?**
	voar <u>mie</u> • erdh <u>kohs</u> • dah ehn
	tahk • sa til <u>loaft</u> • how • nern
I would like to go to...Airport, please.	**Jeg vil gerne til... Lufthavn, tak.**
	yie vil <u>gehr</u> • ner til...<u>loaft</u> • hown tahk
My airline is...	**Jeg skal flyve med...**
	yie skal <u>flew</u> • er medh...

My flight leaves at...	**Mit fly afgår klokken...**
	meet flew <u>ow</u> • gaw <u>kloh</u> • gehrn...
I'm in a rush.	**Jeg har travlt.**
	yie har trowlt
Can you take an alternate route?	**Kan du køre ad en anden rute?**
	kan doo <u>kur</u> • rah adh ehn <u>a</u> • nern <u>roo</u> • ter
Can you drive faster/slower?	**Kan du køre hurtigere/langsommere?**
	kan doo <u>kur</u> • er <u>hoor</u> • dee • ah/ <u>lang</u> • sohm • ah

For Time, see page 23.

YOU MAY SEE...

👁

ANKOMST	arrivals
AFGANG	departures
AFGANGSGATES	departure gates
CHECK-IN SKRANKE	check-in desk
E-BILLET CHECK-IN	e-ticket check-in
BAGAGEBÅND	baggage claim
INDENRIGSFLY	domestic flights
UDENRIGSFLY	international flights

CHECKING IN

Where is the check-in desk for flight...?	**Hvor er check-in skranken for fly...?**
	voar ehr chek • <u>in skrahng</u> • gern foh flew...
My name is...	**Mit navn er...**
	meet nown ehr...
I'm going to...	**Jeg skal til...**
	yie skal til...
I have...	**Jeg har...**
	yie hah

one suitcase	**en kuffert**
	ehn koa • fahd
two suitcases	**to kufferter**
	toh koa • fahd • ehr
one piece of hand luggage	**et styk håndbagage**
	eht stewk hawn • ba • ga • sher
How much luggage is allowed?	**Hvor meget baggage må jeg have med?**
	voar <u>mie</u> • erdh ba • <u>ga</u> • sher mow yie ha medh
Is that pounds or kilos?	**Er det pund eller kilo?**
	ehr deh poon eh • ler kee • loa
Which gate does flight... leave from?	**Hvilken gate afgår fly...fra?**
	<u>vil</u> • gern gayd <u>ow</u> • gaw flew...frah
I'd like a window/ an aisle seat.	**Jeg vil gerne bede om et vinduessæde/ sæde ved midtergangen.**
	yie vil <u>gehr</u> • ner beh ohm ehd
	<u>vin</u> • doos • <u>say</u> • dher/<u>say</u> • dher vedh
	<u>mi</u> • dah • gahng • ern
When do we leave/ arrive?	**Hvornår flyver/ankommer vi?**
	voar • <u>naw flew</u> • ah/<u>an</u> • kohm • ah vee
Is there any delay on the flight...?	**Er fly... forsinket?**
	ehr flew... foh • sing kerdh
How late will it be?	**Hvor forsinket er det?**
	voar foh • <u>sing</u> • kerdh ehr deh

YOU MAY HEAR...

Næste!
nehs • der

Next!

Din billet/Dit pas, tak.
deen bee • lehd/deet pas tahk

Your ticket/
passport, please.

Hvor mange stykker baggage har du?
*voar mahng • er sdur • ger ba • ga • sher
hah doo*

How many pieces
of luggage do you
have?

Du har for meget baggage med.
*doo hah foh mie • erdh ba • ga • sher
mehdh*

You have excess
baggage.

Den er for tung/stor som håndbagage.
*dehn ehr foh toang/stoar som
hawn • ba • ga • sher*

That's too
heavy/large for
a carry-on [to
carry on board].

Har du selv pakket dine tasker?
*hah doo sehl pah • kehrd dee • ner
tas • ger*

Did you pack
these bags
yourself?

Har nogen bedt dig om at tage noget med?
*hah noa • ern behd die ohm ad ta
noa erdh mehdh*

Did anyone give
you anything
to carry?

Tøm dine lommer.
turm dee • ner loh • mah

Empty your
pockets.

Tag dine sko af.
ta dee • ner skoa a

Take off your
shoes.

Nu begynder vi at boarde fly...
noo beh • gur • nah vee ad boar • der flew...

Now boarding
flight...

LUGGAGE

Where is/are...?	**Hvor er...?**
	voar eher...
the luggage trolleys	**bagagevognene**
	ba • ga • sher • vow • nehr • ner
the luggage lockers	**bagageboksene**
	ba • ga • sher • bohk • ser • ner
the baggage claim	**bagagebåndene**
	ba • ga • sher • bawn • er • ner
My luggage has been lost.	**Min bagage er gået tabt.**
	meen ba • ga • sher erh gow • erdh tahbt
My luggage has been stolen.	**Min bagage er blevet stjålet.**
	meen ba • ga • sher erh bleh • verdh stjow • lerdh
My suitcase was damaged.	**Min kuffert er blevet beskadiget.**
	meen koa • fahd erh bleh • verdh beh • ska • dhee • erd

FINDING YOUR WAY

Where is...?	**Hvor er...?**
	voar eher...

the currency exchange office	**vekselkontoret** _vehk_ • serl • kohn • toar • erd
the car hire	**biludlejningen** _beel_ • oodh • lie • ning • ern
the exit	**udgangen** _oodh_ • gahng • ern
the taxi rank	**taxaholdupladsen** _tahk_ • sa • hohl • er • pla • sern
the metro [underground]	**metroen** _meh_ • troa • ern
Is there a bus/train into town?	**Kører der en bus/et tog ind til byen?** _kur_ • rah dehr ehn boos/eht tow in til _bew_ • ern

For Asking Directions, see page 65.

TRAIN

How do I get to the train station?	**Hvordan kommer jeg hen til togstationen?** voar • _dan_ _kom_ • er yie hehn til _tow_ • sta • shoa • nern
Is it far?	**Er det langt herfra?** ehr deh lahngd hehr • _frah_
Where is/are...?	**Hvor er...?** voar ehr...
the ticket office	**billetlugen** bee • _lehd_ • loo • ern
the information desk	**informationslugen** in • foh • ma • _shoans_ • loo • ern
the luggage lockers	**bagageboksene** ba • _ga_ • sher • bohk • ser • ner
the platforms	**perronerne** pehr • _rohng_ • ah • ner

I'd like a schedule [timetable].	**Jeg vil gerne bede om en køreplan.**
	yie vil gehr • ner beh ohm ehn kur • ah • plan
How long is the trip [journey]?	**Hvor længe tager turen?**
	voar layng • er tah too • rern
Is it a direct train?	**Er det et direkte tog?**
	ehr deh ehd dee • reik • ter tow
Do I have to change trains?	**Skal jeg skifte tog?**
	skal yie skeef • der tow
Is the train on time?	**Kommer toget til tiden?**
	koh • mer tow • erdh til teedh • ehn

For Tickets, see page 45.

For Tickets, see page 45.

The Danish train network connects towns across the main islands and the Jutland peninsula. Which train you choose depends on your destination and how quickly you want to get there. **S-bane** or **S-tog** is a commuter train, which serves Copenhagen and surrounding areas. Regional trains and **InterCity** (express) trains travel between Copenhagen and other parts of the country. The **Øresund** train connects Copenhagen and Malmö, Sweden.
A number of discounts are offered depending on the traveler (students, senior citizens, groups, families and children receive considerable reductions), day and time of travel (off-peak times are more highly discounted) as well as the destination. S-trains, the metro and buses run on an integrated network, so you may transfer without paying any additional cost. Keep in mind that buying a **rabatkort** (10-trip ticket), valid for a specified number of zones, is cheaper than buying single tickets. You may also want to consider a 24- hour or 72-hour **CPHCARD** (Copenhagen Card), which offers unlimited train, bus and metro transportation, free entry to over 60 museums and attractions and other discounts. The **CPHCARD** can be purchased online, at tourist offices, in the airport and at major train stations.

DEPARTURES

Which platform does the train to... leave from?	**Fra hvilket spor afgår toget til...?** *frah <u>vil</u> • kerdh spoar <u>ow</u> • gaw <u>tow</u> • erdh til...*
Is this the track [platform] to...?	**Er det her den rigtige perron til...?** *ehr deh hehr dehn <u>rig</u> • tee • er pehr • <u>rohng</u> til...*
Where is track [platform]...?	**Hvor er perron nummer...?** *voar ehr pehr • <u>rohng</u> <u>noa</u> • mah...*
Where do I change for...?	**Hvor skal jeg skifte tog til...?** *voar ska yie <u>skeef</u> • der tow til...*

ON BOARD

Can I sit here/open the window?	**Kan jeg sidde her/åbne vinduet?** *kan yie si • dher hehr/owb • ner vin • doo • eht*
Is this seat taken?	**Er denne siddeplads optaget?** *ehr <u>dehn</u> • er si • dher • plas <u>op</u> • ta • erdh*
I think that's my seat.	**Det er vist min siddeplads.** *deh ehr vist meen si • dher • plas*
Here's my reservation.	**Her er min reservation.** *hehr ehr meen reh • sah • va • shoan*

YOU MAY SEE...

TIL PERRONERNE	to the platforms
INFORMATION	information
PLADSRESERVERINGEN	reservations
ANKOMST	arrivals
AFGANG	departures

BUS

Where's the bus station?	**Hvor ligger busstationen?**
	voar li • gah boos • sta • shoa • nern
How far is it?	**Hvor langt er der?**
	voar langt ehr dehr
How do I get to...?	**Hvordan kommer jeg til...?**
	voar • dan koh • mah yie til...
Does the bus stop at...?	**Stopper bussen ved...?**
	stoh • bah boo • sern vedh...
Can you tell me when to get off?	**Vil du sige til, når jeg skal af?**
	vil doo see • yer til naw yie skal a
Do I have to change buses?	**Er det nødvendigt at skifte bus?**
	ehr deh nurdh vehn • deed ad skeef • der boos

Stop here, please! **Jeg skal af her!**
yie skal a hehr

For Tickets, see page 45.

Danish buses often continue travel where train lines
end. Combining bus and train travel is very easy. You'll
find that many bus stations are located next to train stations,
their arrival and departure schedules are closely timed and
you can use your train ticket to continue your trip on the bus
or vice versa. Taking the bus or combining train and bus travel
is in fact often faster than train-only travel since many bus
connections are more direct than train connections.

YOU MAY HEAR...

Alle i toget! All aboard!
a • ler ee <u>tow</u> • erdh
Billetter, tak. Tickets, please.
bee • <u>lehd</u> • ah tahk
Du skal skifte i... You have to
doo skal <u>skeef</u> • der ee... change at...
Næste stop er... Next stop...
<u>neehs</u> • der stohp ehr...

METRO

Where's the nearest **Hvor er den nærmeste metrostation?**
metro (subway) *voar ehr dehn <u>nehr</u> • meh • ster*
station? *<u>meh</u> • troa • sta • shoan*
Which line for...? **Hvilket tog skal jeg tage til...?**
<u>vil</u> • kerdh tow skal yie ta til...

Which direction?	**Hvilken retning?**
	vil • kern reht • ning
Where do I change for...?	**Hvor skal jeg skifte til...?**
	voar skal yie <u>skeef</u> • der til...
Is this the right train for...?	**Kører det her tog til...?**
	<u>kur</u> • rah deh hehr tow til...
How many stops to...?	**Hvor mange stationer er der til...?**
	voar mahng • er sta • shoa • nehr ehr dehr til
Where are we?	**Hvor er vi henne?**
	voar ehr vee <u>heh</u> • ner

For Finding your Way, see page 52.

Copenhagen's **Metro** (subway) is a clean, quick and convenient way to travel through the city. You can purchase a **rabatkort** (10-trip ticket) or a 24-hour or 72-hour **CPHCARD** (Copenhagen Card) for discounted fares. Tickets for the **Metro** are interchangeable with those for buses and trains. Tickets must be stamped on the platform before boarding. Note that traveling without a valid ticket may lead to a sizeable fine.

BOAT & FERRY

Denmark is comprised of some 500 islands. Though most of the larger islands are linked by bridges, ferries are a way of life in Denmark. There is regular local as well as international ferry service from Denmark to the Baltic States, England, Germany, Norway, Poland and Sweden. Passenger and car reservations can be made in advance via any travel agency.

When is the next boat to…?	**Hvornår går den næste båd til…?** *voar • naw gaw dehn nes • der bowdh til…*
Can I take my car?	**Må jeg tage min bil med?** *mow yie ta meen beel medh*
What time is the next sailing?	**Hvornår afholdes den næste sejlads?** *voar • naw ow • hohl • es dehn neehs • der siy • lahs*
Can I book a seat/cabin?	**Kan jeg booke et sæde/kahyt?** *kan yie book • er eht say • dher/ka • hewt*
How long is the crossing?	**Hvor længe tager overfarten?** *voar layng • ertah ow • ah • fah • dehn*

For Weather, see page 40.

YOU MAY SEE…

REDNINGSBÅD	life boats
REDNINGSVEST	life jackets

TAXI

Taxis can be hailed in the street. Just look for the
FRI (free) sign. Taxis can also be found at taxi stands
at airports and train stations or ordered by phone. All cabs
are metered and service charges are included in the fare,
so tipping is not necessary. Most taxis accept credit cards;
however, if you're not carrying cash, be sure to check first.

Where can I get a taxi?	**Hvor kan jeg få en taxa?**
	voar kan yie fow ehn tahk•sa
Can you send a taxi?	**Kan du sende en taxi?**
	kan doo seh•ner ehn tahk•sa
Do you have the number for a taxi?	**Har du nummeret på en taxi?**
	har doo noa•mahrdh paw ehn tahk•sa
I'd like a taxi now/ for tomorrow at…	**Jeg vil gerne bestille en taxa nu/ til i morgen klokken…**
	yie vil gehr•ner beh•sti•ler ehn tahk•sa noo/til ee moh•wern kloh•gehrn …
Pick me up at (place/time)…	**Hent mig på/klokken…**
	hehnt mie paw/kloh•gehrn…

Please take me to…	**Kør mig til…**
	kur mie til…
this address	**denne adresse**
	deh • ner a • drah • ser
the airport	**lufthavnen**
	loaft • how • nern
the train station	**togstationen**
	tow • sta • shoa • nern
I'm in a hurry.	**Jeg har travlt.**
	yie hah trowlt
Can you drive faster/ slower?	**Kan du køre hurtigere/langsommere?**
	kan doo kur • ah hoor • dee • ah/ lang • sohm • ah
Stop/Wait here.	**Stands/Vent her.**
	stans/vehnd hehr
How much?	**Hvor meget koster det?**
	voar mie • erdh kohs • dah deh
You said…kroner.	**Du sagde…kroner.**
	doo sa • er…kroa • nah
Keep the change.	**Behold byttepengene.**
	beh • hohl bew • der • pchng • ah • ner

YOU MAY HEAR…

Hvor skal du hen?
voar skal doo hehn

Where to?

Hvad er adressen?
vadh ehr a • drah • sern

What's the address?

BICYCLE & MOTORBIKE

(i)

Cycling is very much a part of daily life in Denmark and a regular means of transportation for many Danes. Great investment has been made in recent years to keep Copenhagen bike-friendly, prompting it to be labeled the 'City of Cyclists' of late. Bikes may be borrowed, free of charge, at one of the approximately 125 City Bike Parking spots around the city. All you have to do is leave a deposit that is returned to you when you bring the bike back to any City Bike Parking rack.

I'd like to hire...	**Jeg vil gerne leje...**
	yie vil <u>gehr</u> • ner <u>lie</u> • er...
a bicycle	**en cykel**
	ehn <u>sew</u> • gerl
a moped	**en knallert**
	ehn <u>kna</u> • lahd
a motorcycle	**en motorcykel**
	ehn <u>moa</u> • tah • sew • gerl
How much per day/ week?	**Hvad koster det per dag/uge?**
	vadh <u>kohs</u> • dah deh pehr da/<u>oo</u> • er
Can I have a helmet/ lock?	**Kan jeg få en hjelm/lås?**
	kan yie fow ehn yehlm/lows

CAR HIRE

Where can I hire a car?	**Hvor kan jeg leje en bil?**
	voar kan yie <u>lie</u> • er ehn beel
I'd like to hire...	**Jeg vil gerne leje...**
	yie vil <u>gehr</u> • ner <u>lie</u> • er...

a cheap/small car	**en billig/lille bil**
	ehn bee • lee/lee • ler beel
a 2-door/	**en to-dørs/fire-dørs bil**
4-door car	*ehn toa • durs/feer • durs beel*
an automatic	**en bil med automatgear**
	ehn beel mehdh ow • toa • mad geer
a manual car	**almindeligt gear**
	al • meen • deh • leet geer
a car with air-	**en bil med klimaanlæg**
conditioning	*ehn beel medh klee • ma • an • layg*
a car seat	**et barnesæde**
	eht bah • ner • say • dher
How much is it...?	**Hvor meget koster det...?**
	voar mie • erdh kohs • dah deh...
per day/week	**per dag/uge**
	pehr da/oo • er
per kilometer	**per kilometer**
	pehr kee • loa • meh • dah
for unlimited	**med ubegrænset kørsel**
mileage	*medh oo • beh • grehn • serdh kur • sehl*
with insurance	**med forsikring**
	medh foh • sik • ring
Are there any	**Er der nogen specialtilbud...?**
discounts for...?	*ehr dehr noa • ern speh • shal • til • boodh...*

YOU MAY HEAR...

Har du et internationalt kørekort?
har doo et <u>in</u>•tah•na•shoa•nalt
<u>kur</u>•rah•kawd

Do you have an international driver's license?

Må jeg se dit pas?
mow yie seh deet pas

May I see your passport?

Ønsker du at tegne forsikring?
<u>urn</u>•sgah doo ad <u>tie</u>•ner for•<u>sik</u>•ring

Do you want insurance?

Du skal betale et depositum på...
doo skal beh•<u>ta</u>•ler eht
deh•<u>poa</u>•see•toam paw...

There's a deposit of...

Underskriv venligst her.
<u>vehn</u>•leesd hehr

Sign here.

FUEL STATION

YOU MAY SEE...

95 OKTAN	regular
98 OKTAN	super
DIESEL	diesel

Where's the nearest fuel station?	**Hvor er den nærmeste benzinstation?** *voar ehr dehn <u>nehr</u>•mer•ster behn•<u>seen</u>•sta•shoan*
Fill it up, please.	**Fuld tank, tak.** *fool tahnk tahk*
... liters, please.	**...liter benzin.** *...<u>lee</u>•dah behn•<u>seen</u>*

| I'd like to pay in cash/by credit card. | **Jeg vil gerne betale kontant/ med kreditkort.** |
| | *yie vil <u>gehr</u> • ner beh • <u>ta</u> • ler kohn • <u>tant</u>/ mehdh kreh • <u>deet</u> • kawd* |

For Numbers, see page 20.

ASKING DIRECTIONS

Are we on the right road for...?	**Er det den rette vej til...?**
	ehr deh dehn <u>reh</u> • der vie til...
How far is it to...?	**Hvor langt er der til...?**
	voar lahngt ehr dehr til...
Where's...?	**Hvor er...?**
	voar ehr...
...Street	**...gade ...**
	<u>ga</u> • dher
this address	**denne adresse**
	<u>deh</u> • ner ah • <u>drah</u> • ser
the highway [motorway]	**motorvejen**
	<u>moa</u> • tah • vie • ern
Can you show me on the map?	**Kan du vise mig det på kortet?**
	kan doo <u>vee</u> • ser mie deh paw <u>kaw</u> • derdh

I'm lost.	**Jeg er faret vild.**
	yie ehr <u>fah</u> • erdh veel zeen

PARKING

Parking in Denmark is restricted. Metered zones allow
up to three hours of parking. In Copenhagen, in unmetered
zones, there are ticket vending machines where you can pay
with coins and bills or by credit card. The ticket should be in
a visible place on the dashboard of your car.

Is there a parking lot [car park] nearby?	**Er der en parkeringsplads i nærheden?**
	ehr dehr ehn pah • <u>keh</u> • rings • plas ee <u>nehr</u> • heh • dhern
Can I park here?	**Må jeg parkere her?**
	mow yie pah • <u>keh</u> • ah hehr
Where's the parking garage/parking meter?	**Hvor er parkeringsgaragen/ parkometeret?**
	voar ehr pah • keh • rings • gah • rah • ghehn pah • ko • meh • dah • reht
How much is it…?	**Hvor meget koster det…?**
	voar <u>mie</u> • erdh <u>kohs</u> • dah deh…
per hour	**per time**
	pehr <u>tee</u> • mer
per day	**per dag**
	pehr da
overnight	**for natten**
	foh <u>na</u> • dern

YOU MAY HEAR...

igeud
lee • er • oodh
straight ahead

til venstre
til vehn • sdrah
on the left

til højre
til hoi • ah
on the right

på/rundt om hjørnet
paw/roundt ohm yur • nerdh
on/around the corner

overfor...
ow • ah • foh...
opposite...

bagved...
ba • vehdh...
behind...

ved siden af...
vehdh see • dhern a...
next to...

efter...
ehf • dah...
after...

nord/syd
noar/sewdh
north/south

øst/vest
ursd/vehsd
east/west

ved trafiklyset
vedh trah • feeg • lew • serdh
at the traffic light

ved vejkrydset
vehdh vie • krew • serdh
at the intersection

BREAKDOWN & REPAIR

My car broke down/
won't start.

Min bil har fået motorstop/vil ikke starte.
*meen beel har fow • erdh
moa • tah • stohb/vil ig • ger stah • der*

Can you fix it (today)?	**Kan du reparere den (i dag)?**
	kan doo reh • pah • <u>rehr</u> dehn (ee • dah)
When will it be ready?	**Hvornår er den klar?**
	voar • <u>naw</u> ehr dehn klah
How much?	**Hvor meget koster det?**
	voar <u>mie</u> • erdh <u>kohs</u> • dah deh
I have a puncture/ flat tyre (tire).	**Jeg har et punkteret/fladt dæk.**
	yie har ehd punh • te • rehd/fladht deck

For Time, see page 23.

ACCIDENTS

There's been an accident.	**Der er sket en ulykke.**
	dehr ehr skeht ehn <u>oo</u> • lew • ger
Call an ambulance/ the police.	**Ring hurtigt efter en ambulance/ politiet.**
	ring <u>hoor</u> • deet <u>ehf</u> • dah ehn
	ahm • boo • <u>lahng</u> • ser/poa • lee • <u>tee</u> • erdl

For Police, see page 137.

PLACES TO STAY

NEED TO KNOW

Can you recommend a hotel?
Kan du anbefale et hotel?
kan doo <u>an</u> • beh • fa • ler eht hoa • <u>tehl</u>

I have a reservation.
Jeg har bestilt værelse.
yie har beh • <u>stild</u> <u>vehrl</u> • ser

My name is…
Mit navn er…
meet nown ehr…

Do you have a room…?
Har I et værelse…?
har ee ehd <u>vehrl</u> • ser…

  for one/two
enkeltværelse/dobbeltværelse
<u>ehn</u> • kerld • vehrl • ser/ <u>doh</u> • berld • vehrl • ser

  with a bathroom
med bad
mehdh badh

  with air conditioning
med klimaanlæg
mehdh <u>klee</u> • ma • an • layg

  for tonight
for i nat
for ee nad

  for two nights
for to nætter
for toa <u>nay</u> • dah

  for one week
for en uge
for ehn <u>oo</u> • er

How much?
Hvor meget koster det?
voar <u>mie</u> • erdh <u>kohs</u> • dah deh

Do you have anything cheaper?
Har du noget billigere?
har doo <u>noa</u> • erdh <u>bee</u> • leer

When's check-out?
Hvornår skal vi tjekke ud?
voar • <u>naw</u> skal vee <u>tjeh</u> • ker oodh

Can I leave this in the safe?	**Må jeg lade dette være i boksen?**
	mow yie la deh • ter vay • er i bohk • sern
Can I leave my bags?	**Må jeg lade mine tasker være her?**
	mow yie la mee • ner tas • gah vay • ah hehr
Can I have the bill/ a receipt?	**Kan jeg få regningen/en kvittering?**
	kan yie fow rie • ning • ern/ehn kvee • teh • ring
I'll pay in cash/by credit card.	**Jeg vil gerne betale kontant/med kreditkort.**
	yie vil gehr • ner beh • ta • ler kohn • tahnt/ mehdh kreh • deet • kawd

SOMEWHERE TO STAY

Can you recommend...?	**Kan du anbefale ...?**
	kan doo an • beh • fa • ler
a hotel	**et hotel**
	eht hoa • tehl
a hostel	**et hostel**
	ehd hos • tehl

a campsite	**en campingplads**
	ehn kahm • ping • plas
a bed and	**et bed and breakfast**
breakfast	*ehd bed and breakfast*
What is it near?	**Hvad ligger det i nærheden af?**
	vadh li • gah deh ee nehr • heh • dhern a
How do I get there?	**Hvordan kommer jeg derhen?**
	voar • dan koh • mer yie dehr • hehn

AT THE HOTEL

I have a reservation.	**Jeg har en reservation.**
	yie hah ehn reh • sah • va • shoan
My name is…	**Mit navn er…**
	meet nown ehr…
Do you have	**Har I et ledigt værelse…?**
a room…?	*hah ee edh leh • dheed vehrl • ser…*
with a toilet/	**med toilet/brusebad**
shower	*medh toa • ee • lehd/broo • ser • badh*
with a bathroom	**med bad**
	mehdh badh
with air	**med klimaanlæg**
conditioning	*mehdh klee • ma • an • layg*
that's smoking/	**ryger/ikke-ryger**
non-smoking	*rew • ah/ig • ger rew • ah*
for tonight	**for i nat**
	foh ee nad
for two nights	**for to nætter**
	foh toa nay • dah
for one week	**for en uge**
	foh ehn oo • er
Does the hotel	**Har hotellet…?**
have…?	*hah hoa • tehl • erdh…*
a computer	**en pc**
	ehn peh seh

an elevator [a lift]	**en elevator**
	ehn eh • ler • va • toh
(wireless) internet	**(trådløst) internet**
	(trowdh • lurst) in • tah • neht
room service	**service på værelset**
	sur • vees paw vehrl • serdh
a gym	**et motions center**
	ehd moa • shoan • sehn • dah
I need...	**Jeg skal bruge...**
	yie skal broo • er...
an extra bed	**en ekstra seng**
	ehn ehk • strah sehng
a cot	**en klapseng**
	ehn klahp • sehng
a crib	**en barneseng**
	ehn bah • ner • sehng

In Denmark, there is a variety of places to stay in
addition to hotels, which range from one to five stars.
You could choose to stay in a bed and breakfast, such as a
kro (country inn), in an old **slot** (castle) or a **motel** (motel).
If you are traveling by car, good options include **vandrerhjem**
(a hostel), **ungdomsherberg** (a student hotel) or **sommerhus**
(a summer house), which refers to any rented living space,
such as a seaside cottage or apartment. For a unique vacation
experience, you might choose a **bondegårdsferie** (farmhouse
stay), which lets you taste Danish farm life firsthand.
Advanced reservations are recommended particularly
during the high season. If you arrive in Denmark without a
reservation, tourist information offices can assist in locating
places to stay as can the Room Reservation Service, found at
Central Train Station in Copenhagen.

YOU MAY HEAR...

Må jeg bede om dit pas/kreditkort.
mow yie beh ohm deet pas/
kreh • deet • kawd
Udfyld venligst denne formular.
oodh • fewl vehn • leesd deh • ner foh • moo • lah
Underskriv venligst her.
oa • nah • sgreew vehn • leesd hehr

Your passport/
credit card,
please.
Fill out this form.

Sign here.

PRICE

How much per night/week?	**Hvad koster det per nat/uge?** *vadh kohs • dah deh pehr nad/oo • er*
Does the price include breakfast/ sales tax [VAT]?	**Inkluderer prisen morgenmad/moms?** *in • kloo • deh • ah pree • sern mawn • madh/mawms*
Are there any discounts?	**Kan jeg fĺ rabat?** *kan yie fow rah • badh*

PREFERENCES

Can I see the room?	**Må jeg se værelset?** *mow yie seh vehrl • serdh*
I'd like a...room.	**Jeg vil gerne have et ... værelse.** *yie vil gehr • ner ha ehd... vehrl • ser.*
better	**bedre** *bedh • rah*
bigger	**større** *stur • rah*
cheaper	**billigere** *bee • leer*

quieter	**mere roligt**
	meh • rah roh • lidt
I'll take it.	**Jeg tager det.**
	yie tah deh
No, I won't take it.	**Nej, jeg vil ikke have det.**
	nie, yie vil ig • ger ha deh

QUESTIONS

Where's…?	**Hvor er…?**
	voar ehr…
the bar	**baren**
	<u>bah</u> • ern
the restroom [toilet]	**toilettet**
	toa • ee • <u>leh</u> • derdh
the elevator [lift]	**elevatoren**
	eh • ler • <u>va</u> • tohn
Can I have…?	**Kan jeg få…?**
	kan yie fow…
a blanket	**et tæppe**
	eht <u>teh</u> • ber
an iron	**et strygejern**
	eht <u>strew</u> • er • yehrn

the room key/ key card	**nøglen/kortet til værelset**
	noi • lern/kaw • derdh til vehrl • serdh
a pillow	**en pude**
	ehn poo • dher
soap	**noget sæbe**
	noa • erdh say • ber
toilet paper	**noget toiletpapir**
	noa • erdh toa • ee • led • pah • peer
a towel	**et håndklæde**
	eht hawn • klay • dher
Do you have an adapter for this?	**Har I en adapter til denne her?**
	har ee ehn a • dahp • tah til deh • ner hehr
How do I turn on the lights?	**Hvordan tænder jeglyset?**
	voar • dan tay • ner yie lew • serdh
Can you wake me at…?	**Kan du vække mig klokken…?**
	kan doo vay • ger mie klohg • gehrn…
Can I have my things from the safe?	**Må jeg få mine ting i boksen?**
	mow yie fow mee • ner ting ee bohk • sern
Is there any mail/a message for me?	**Er der noget post/nogen beskeder til mig?**
	ehr dehr noa • erdh pohst/noa • ern beh • sgeh • dhah til mie
Do you have a laundry service?	**Har I vasketøjsservice?**
	hah ee vas • ger • turys • sur • vees

YOU MAY SEE...	
SKUB/TRÆK	push/pull
TOILET	restroom [toilet]
BRUSER	shower
ELEVATOREN	elevator [lift]
TRAPPE	stairs
VASKERI	laundry
VIL IKKE FORSTYRRES	do not disturb
BRANDDØR	fire door
NØDUDGANG	emergency exit
MORGENVÆKNING	wake-up call

PROBLEMS

There's a problem.	**Der er et problem.**
	dehr ehr eht proa • blehm
I've lost my key/key card.	**Jeg har tabt min nøgle/mit nøglekort.**
	yie hah tahbd meen <u>noi</u> • ler/meet <u>noi</u> • ler • kawd
I've locked myself out of my room.	**Jeg har låst mig ude af mit værelse.**
	yie hah lowsd mie <u>oo</u> • dher a meet vehrl • ser
There's no hot water/ toilet paper.	**Der er ikke noget varmt vand/ toiletpapir.**
	dehr ehr <u>ig</u> • ger noa • erdh vahmd van/toa • ee • <u>lehd</u> • pah • peer
The room is dirty.	**Værelset er beskidt.**
	<u>vehrl</u> • serdh ehr beh • <u>skeed</u>
There are bugs in our room.	**Der er insekter på værelset.**
	dehr ehr in • <u>sehg</u> • tah paw <u>vehrl</u> • serd
...doesn't work.	**...er i uorden.**
	...ehr ee <u>oo</u> • oh • dern

Can you fix...?	**Kan du reparere...?**
	kan doo reh • pah • <u>reh</u> • ah...
the air-conditioning	**klimaanlægget**
	<u>klee</u> • ma • an • layg
the fan	**ventilatoren**
	vehn • tee • la • shoan
the heat [heating]	**varmen**
	<u>vah</u> • mern
the light	**lyset**
	<u>lew</u> • serdh
the TV	**fjernsynet**
	<u>fyehrn</u> • sew • nerdh
the toilet	**toilettet**
	toa • ee • <u>leh</u> • derdh
Can I get another room?	**Kan jeg få et andet værelse?**
	can yie fow eht <u>an</u> • erdh <u>vehrl</u> • ser

Danish electricity is generally 220 volts, though many camping sites also have 110-volt plugs available. British and American appliances will need an adapter.

CHECKING OUT

When do I have to check out?	**Hvornår skal jeg tjekke ud?**
	voar • <u>naw</u> skal yie <u>tyay</u> • ger oodh
Can I leave my bags here until...?	**Må jeg lade mine tasker stå her indtil...?**
	mow yie la <u>mee</u> • ner <u>tas</u> • gah stow hehr <u>in</u> • til...
Can I have an itemized bill/a receipt?	**Må jeg bede om en udspecificeret regning/kvittering?**
	mow yie beh ohm ehn oodh • speh • see • fee • seh • redh <u>rie</u> • ning/kvee • <u>teh</u> • ring

I think there's a mistake in this bill.	**Jeg tror, der er en fejl i regningen.**
	yie troar dehr ehr ehn fiel ee rie • ning • ern
I'll pay in cash/by credit card.	**Jeg vil gerne betale kontant/med kreditkort.**
	yie vil <u>gehr</u> • ner beh • <u>ta</u> • ler kohn • <u>tant</u>/mehdh kreh • <u>deet</u> • kawd

---

ⓘ

In Denmark, **moms** (sales tax or value-added tax) and service charges are included in your bill in hotels and restaurants, in admissions charges and purchase prices as well as taxi fares. Tips may be given for outstanding service, but they are not necessary.

RENTING

I've reserved an apartment/a room.	**Jeg har reserveret en lejlighed/et værelse.**
	yie hah reh • sah • <u>veh</u> • rerdh ehn lie • lee • hehdh/eht <u>vehrl</u> • ser
My name is...	**Mit navn er...**
	meet nown ehr...
Can I have the key/ key card?	**Må jeg bede om nøglen/nøglekortet?**
	mow yie beh ohm <u>noi</u> • lern/ <u>noi</u> • ler • kaw • derdh
Are there...?	**Findes der...?**
	<u>fin</u> • ners dehr...
dishes	**spisestel**
	<u>spee</u> • ser • stehl
pillows	**puder**
	<u>poo</u> • dhah
sheets	**lagener**
	<u>la</u> • ner

towels	**håndklæder** _hawn_ • klay • dhah
kitchen utensils	**køkkenredskaber** kur • ken • redh • skab • ah
When/Where do I put out the bins/recycling?	**Hvornår/Hvor skal jeg sætte skraldet ud/genbrug?** voar • _naw_/voar skal yie _seh_ • der skrah • _lerdh_ oodh/gehn • broo oodh
… is broken.	**…er i uorden.** …ehr ee _oo_ • oh • dern
How does…work?	**Hvordan fungerer…?** voar • _dan_ fung • _geh_ • rah…
the air conditioner	**klimaanlægget** _klee_ • ma • an • lay • gerdh
the dishwasher	**opvaskemaskinen** _ohb_ • va • sker • ma • skee • nern
the freezer	**fryseren** _frew_ • sern
the heater	**varmen** _vah_ • mern
the microwave	**mikroovnen** _mee_ • kroa • ow • nern
the refrigerator	**køleskabet** _kur_ • ler • ska • berdh

the stove	**ovnen**
	_ow_ • nern
the washing	**vaskemaskinen**
machine	_vas_ • ger • ma • skee • nern

DOMESTIC ITEMS

I need…	**Jeg skal bruge…**
	yie skal _broo_ • er…
an adapter	**en adapter**
	ehn a • _dahb_ • dah
aluminum foil	**aluminiumsfolie**
	a • loo • _mee_ • nee • oums • foal • yer
a bottle opener	**en oplukker**
	ehn _ohb_ • loa • ger
a broom	**en kost**
	ehn kowsd
I need…	**Jeg skal bruge…**
	yie skal _broo_ • er…
a can opener	**en dåseåbner**
	ehn _dow_ • ser • _owb_ • nah
cleaning supplies	**rengøringsartikler**
	rehn • gur • rings • ah • teek • lah
a corkscrew	**en proptrækker**
	ehn _prohb_ • tray • gah
detergent	**vaskemiddel**
	vas • ker • _mee_ • dherl
dishwashing liquid	**opvaskemiddel**
	ohb • vas • ker • mee • dherl
bin bags	**skraldeposer**
	skrah • ler • poa • sah
a light bulb	**en pære**
	ehn _pay_ • ah
matches	**tændstikker**
	tehn • sti • kah

a mop	**en moppe**
	ehn <u>moh</u> • ber
napkins	**papirservietter**
	pah • <u>peer</u> • sehr • vee • <u>eh</u> • dah
paper towels	**papirhåndklæder**
	pah • <u>peer</u> • hawn • klay • dhah
plastic wrap	**plastfolie**
[cling film]	*<u>plast</u> • foal • yer*
a plunger	**en svupper**
	ehn swob • ah
scissors	**en saks**
	ehn saks
a vacuum cleaner	**en støvsuger**
	ehn <u>sturw</u> • soo • ah

For In the Kitchen, see page 193.

AT THE HOSTEL

Do you have any places left for tonight?	**Har I nogen ledige pladser i nat?**
	hah ee <u>noa</u> • ern <u>leh</u> • dhi • yer
	<u>plas</u> • sah ee nad
Can I have...?	**Kan jeg få...?**
	kan yie fow...
a single/double room	**et enkeltværelse/dobbeltværelse**
	eht <u>ehn</u> • kerld • vehrl • ser/
	<u>doh</u> • berld • vehrl • ser
a blanket	**et tæppe**
	eht <u>tay</u> • ber
a pillow	**en pude**
	ehn <u>poo</u> • dher
sheets	**lagener**
	la • ner
soap	**sæbe**
	<u>say</u> • ber

towels	**håndklæder**
	hawn • klay • dhah
Do you have lockers?	**Har I aflåste skabe?**
	hah ee aw • lowsd • er ska • ber
What time do you lock up?	**Hvornår lukker I for natten?**
	voar • naw loa • gah ee foh nad • dern
Do I need a membership card?	**Skal man have et medlemskort?**
	skal man hah ehd medh • lems • kawd
Here's my international student card.	**Her er mit internationale studiekort.**
	hehr ehr meet in • tah • na • shoa • naleh stu • dyie • kawd

ⓘ

Known as **DANHOSTEL, Danmarks Vandrerhjem**, the Danish Youth Hostel Association operates official youth hostels throughout Denmark. You may request a private or shared room. The charge covers only the cost of the room; additional fees apply for bed linens and/or breakfast. Hostelling International (HI) cardholders are exempt from surcharges and receive special discounts. HI membership cards can be purchased on the spot.

GOING CAMPING

Can we camp here?	**Kan vi campere her?**
	kan vee kahm • peh • ah hehr
Is there a campsite near here?	**Er der en campingplads i nærheden?**
	ehr dehr ehn kahm • ping • plas ee nehr • heh • dhern
What is the charge per day/week?	**Hvad koster det per dag/uge?**
	vadh kohs • dah deh pehr da/oo • er
Are there...?	**Er der...?**
	ehr dehr...
cooking facilities	**køkkenfaciliteter**
	kur • ken • fa • see • lee • teh • dah
electrical outlets	**stikkontakter**
	stik • kohn • tahg • dah
laundry facilities	**vaskerum**
	vas • ger • roam
showers	**brusebad**
	broo • ser • badh
tents for hire	**telte til leje**
	tehl • der til lie • er
Where can I empty the chemical toilet?	**Hvor kan jeg tømme det kemiske toilet?**
	voar kan yie tur • mer deh keh • mis • ger toa • ee • lehd

For In the Kitchen, see page 193.

YOU MAY SEE...

DRIKKEVAND	drinking water
CAMPING FORBUDT	no camping
BÅLTÆNDING/ GRILLNING FORBUDT	no fires/barbecues

COMMUNICATIONS

NEED TO KNOW

Where's an internet cafe?	**Hvor ligger der en internetcafé?** *voar li • gah dehr ehn* *in • tah • neht • ca • feh*
Can I access the internet here/ check e-mail?	**Kan jeg gå på internettet herfra/ tjekke min e-mail?** *kan yie gow paw in • tah • neh • derdh* *hehr • frah/tjay • ker meen ee • mail*
How much per hour/ half hour?	**Hvor meget koster det per time/ halve time?** *voar mie • erdh kohs • dah deh pehr* *tee • mer/hal • ver tee • mer*
How do I connect/ log on?	**Hvordan kobler/logger jeg mig på?** *voar • dan kohb • lah/lohg • ah yie mie* *paw*
I'd like a phone card, please.	**Jeg vil gerne have et telefonkort, tak.** *yie vil gehr • ner ha eht* *teh • ler • foan • kawd tahk*
Can I have your phone number?	**Kan jeg få dit telefonnummer?** *kan yie fow deet* *teh • ler • foan • noa • mer*
Here's my number/ e-mail address.	**Her er mit telefonnumer/min e-mail- adresse.** *hehr ehr meet teh • ler • foan • noa • mer/* *meen ee • mail • a • drah • ser*
Call me.	**Ring til mig.** *ring til mie*
E-mail me.	**Send mig en e-mail.** *sehn mie ehn ee • mail*

Hello. This is…	**Hallo. Det er…**
	ha • loa deh ehr…
I'd like to speak to…	**Jeg vil gerne tale med…**
	yie vil gehr • ner ta • ler medh…
Can you repeat that?	**Kan du gentage det?**
	kan doo gehn • ta deh
I'll call back later.	**Jeg ringer tilbage senere.**
	yie ring • ah til • ba • yer seh • nah
Bye.	**Farvel.**
	fah • vehl
Where's the post office?	**Hvor ligger posthuset?**
	voar li • gah pohsd • hoo • serdh
I'd like to send this to…	**Jeg vil gerne sende dette til…**
	yie vil gehr • ner seh • ner deh • der til…

ONLINE

Where's an internet cafe?	**Hvor ligger der en internetcafé?**
	voar li • gah dehr ehn in • tah • neht • ca • feh
Does it have wireless internet?	**Har den trådløst internet?**
	hah dehn trowdh • lurst in • tah • net
What is the WiFi password?	**Hvad er WiFi-passwordet?**
	vadh her WiFi-pass • word • edh
Is the WiFi free?	**Er der gratis WiFi?**
	ehr dehr ghra • tis WiFi
Do you have bluetooth?	**Har I bluetooth?**
	hahr ee bluetooth?
How do I turn the computer on/off?	**Hvordan tænder/slukker jeg for computeren?**
	voar • dan tay • nah/sloa • gah yie foh cohm • pew • dern

Can I...?	**Kan jeg...?**
	kan yie...
access the	**gå på internettet herfra**
internet here	*gow paw in • tah • neh • derdh hehr • frah*
check e-mail	**tjekke min e-mail**
	tjay • ker meen ee • mail
print	**printe**
	prin • ter
plug in/charge my	**oplade min bærbare/iPhone/iPad/**
laptop/iPhone/	**BlackBerry**
iPad/BlackBerry	*ohb • la • der meen behr • barer/iPhone/*
	iPad/BlackBerry
access Skype	**bruge Skype**
	broo • er Skype
How much per hour/	**Hvor meget koster det per time/halve**
half hour?	**time?**
	voar mie • erdh kohs • dah deh pehr
	tee • mer/hal • ver tee • mer
How do I...?	**Hvordan....?**
	voar • dan...
connect/	**kobler jeg mig på/fra**
disconnect	*kohb • lah yie mie paw/frah*
log on/off	**logger jeg på/af**
	lohg • ah yie paw/a

type this symbol	**indtaster jeg dette symbol** *in • tas • dah yie deh • der sewm • boal*
What's your e-mail?	**Hvad er din e-mail adresse?** *vadh ehr deen ee • mail • a • drah • ser*
My e-mail is…	**Min e-mail adresse er…** *meen ee • mail • a • drah • ser ehr…*
Do you have a scanner?	**Har I en scanner?** *hah ee ehn scan • ner*

YOU MAY SEE…

E-MAIL	e-mail
FORLAD	exit
HJÆLP	help
INSTANT MESSENGER	instant messenger
INTERNET	internet
LOG IND	login
NY (BESKED)	new (message)
UDSKRIV	print
BRUGERNAVN/ADGANGSKODE	username/ password
TRÅDLØS INTERNETFORBINDELSE	wireless internet

SOCIAL MEDIA

Are you on Facebook/ Twitter?	**Er du på Facebook/Twitter?** *her doo paw Facebook/Twitter*
What's your user name?	**Hvad er dit brugernavn?** *vadh ehr deet broo • er • nown*
I'll add you as a friend.	**Jeg vil tilføje dig som ven.** *yie vil til • foi • er die som vehn*

I'll follow you on Twitter.	**Jeg vil følge dig på Twitter.** *yie vil foil • ier die paw Twitter*
Are you following...?	**Følger du ...?** *foil • ier doo*
I'll put the pictures on Facebook/Twitter.	**Jeg vil lægge billederne op på Facebook/Twitter.** *yie vil lay • ger bee • leh • ar op paw Facebook/Twitter*
I'll tag you in the pictures.	**Jeg vil tagge dig på billederne.** *yie vil tag • ge die paw bee • leh • arner*

PHONE

A phone card/ prepaid phone, please.	**Jeg vil gerne have et telefonkort/ taletidskort, tak.** *yievil <u>gehr</u> • ner ha ehd teh • ler • <u>foan</u> • kawd/ ta • ler • teedhs • kawd tahk*
How much?	**Hvor meget koster det?** *voar <u>mie</u> • erdh <u>kohs</u> • dah deh*
Where's the pay phone?	**Hvor er mønttelefonen?** *voar ehr murnhd • teh • ler • foan*
What's the area/ country code for...?	**Hvad er områdenummeret/landekoden for...?** *vadh ehr <u>ohm</u> • row • dhe • noa • mahrdh/ <u>la</u> • ner • koa • dher foh...*
What's the number for Information?	**Hvad er nummeret til nummeroplysningen?** *vadh ehr <u>noa</u> • mahrdh til <u>noa</u> • mah • ohb • <u>lews</u> • ning • ern*
I'd like the number for...	**Jeg vil gerne bede om nummeret til...** *yie vil <u>gehr</u> • ner beh ohm <u>noa</u> • mahrdh til...*
I'd like to call collect [reverse the charges].	**Jeg vil gerne ringe med modtager betaler.** *yie vil gehr • ner ring • er medh moadh • ta • ehr beh • ta • lar*

My phone doesn't work here.	**Min telefon virker ikke her.**
	meen teh • ler • <u>foan</u> <u>veer</u> • gah ig • ger hehr
What network are you on?	**Hvilket netværk er du på?**
	vil • gerdh net • vehrk ehr doo paw
Is it 3G?	**Er det 3G?**
	ehr deh 3G
I have run out of credit/minutes.	**Jeg har ikke mere taletid.**
	yie hah ig • ger meh • rah ta • ler • teedh
Can I buy some credit?	**Kan jeg købe taletidskort her?**
	kan yie kur • ber ta • ler • teedhs • kawd hehr
Do you have a phone charger?	**Har du en telefonoplader?**
	hah doo ehn te • ler • foan • op • la • dher
Can I have your number?	**Må jeg få dit nummer?**
	mow yie fow deet <u>noa</u> • mah
My number is…	**Mit nummer er…**
	meet <u>noa</u> • mah ehr…
Call me.	**Ring venligst til mig.**
	ring <u>vehn</u> • leest til mie
Text me.	**Send mig venligst en tekstbesked.**
	sehn mie <u>vehn</u> • leest ehn <u>tehkst</u> • beh • skehdh

I'll call you.	**Jeg ringer til dig.**
	yie <u>ring</u>•ah til die
I'll text you.	**Jeg sender dig en tekstbesked.**
	yie <u>sehn</u>•ah die ehn <u>tehkst</u>•beh•skehdh

YOU MAY HEAR...

Hvem er det?	Who's calling?
vehm ehr deh	
Vær rar og vent.	Hold on.
vehr rah ow <u>vehn</u>•der	
Han/Hun kan ikke komme til telefonen.	He/She can't
han/hoon kan <u>ig</u>•ger <u>koh</u>•mer til teh•ler•<u>foa</u>•nern	come to the phone.
Ønsker du at lægge en besked?	Would you like to
<u>urn</u>•sgah doo ad <u>lay</u>•ger ehn beh•<u>skehdh</u>	leave a message?
Kan han/hun ringe tilbage til dig?	Can he/she call
kan han/hoon <u>ring</u>•er til <u>ba</u>•yer til die	you back?
Hvad er dit telefonnummer?	What's your
vadh ehr deet teh•ler•<u>foan</u>•noa•mah	number?

PHONE ETIQUETTE

Hello. This is...	**Hallo. Det er...**
	ha•<u>loa</u> deh ehr...
I'd like to speak to...	**Jeg vil gerne tale med...**
	yie vil <u>gehr</u>•ner ta•ler mehdh...
Extension...	**Lokal...**
	loa•<u>kal</u>...
Speak louder/more slowly, please.	**Vær rar og tal lidt højere/lidt langsommere.**
	vehr rah ow ta•ler lit <u>hoi</u>•ah/lit <u>lang</u>•sohm•ah

In Denmark, public phones either accept coins or prepaid phone cards. For coin-operated phones, once the line is engaged — even if it is busy — your coin will not be returned, so start with a low denomination coin. Prepaid phone cards can be purchased in post offices and kiosks. The price per call from a public phone is twice that from a private line but some kiosks allow you to make calls with a cheaper international rate using prepaid phone cards. Calls can also be made from the TelecomCenter at Central Train Station in Copenhagen.

Important telephone numbers:

emergencies, 112
information, 118
operator assistance, 113

To call the U.S. or Canada from Denmark, dial 00 + 1 + area code + phone number. To call the U.K., dial 00 + 44 + area code (minus the first 0) + phone number.

Can you repeat that? **Kan du gentage det?**
kan doo <u>gehn</u> • ta deh

I'll call back later. **Jeg ringer tilbage senere.**
yie <u>ring</u> • ah til • <u>ba</u> • yer <u>seh</u> • nah

Bye.	**Farvel.** *fah • vehl*

FAX

Can I send/receive a fax here?	**Kan jeg sende/modtage en fax her?** *kan yie sehn • ner/moadh • ta ehn fahks hehr*
What's the fax number?	**Hvad er faxnummeret?** *vadh ehr fahks • noa • mahrdh*
Fax this to…	**Fax venligst dette til…** *fahks vehn • leesd deh • ter til…*

POST

(i)

The regular hours of operation of post offices in
Denmark are Monday to Friday from 10:00 a.m. to 5:30
p.m. and Saturday 10:00 a.m. to 1:00 p.m.; hours in the
provinces may vary. Mailboxes are red and, like post office
signs, display an embossed crown-and-arrow logo and **POST**
in white.

Where's the post office/mailbox?	**Hvor ligger posthuset/er postkassen?** *voar li • gah pohst • hoo • serdh/ehr pohst • ka • sern*
A stamp for this letter/postcard, please.	**Jeg vil gerne have et frimærke til dette brev/postkort, tak.** *yie vil gehr • ne ha eht free • mehr • ker til deh • der brehw/pohst • kawd tahk*
How much?	**Hvor meget koster det?** *voar mie • erdh kohs • dah deh*

I'd like to send this package by airmail/express.	**Jeg vil gerne sende denne pakke med luftpost/ekspres.**
	yie vil gehr • ner sehn • ner deh • ner pah • ker mehdh loaft • pohst/ehks • prehs
Can I have receipt?	**Kan jeg få en kvittering?**
	kan yie fow ehn kvee • teh • ring

SIGHTSEEING

NEED TO KNOW

Where's the tourist information office?	**Hvor ligger turistinformationen?**
	voar li • gah too • reest • in • foh • ma • shoa • nern
What are the main points of interest?	**Hvad er de vigtigste seværdigheder?**
	vadh ehr dee vig • tee • ster seh • vehr • dee • heh • dhah
Do you offer tours in English?	**Tilbyder I turer på engelsk?**
	til • bew • dhah ee too • ah paw ehng • erlsk
Can I have a map/guide?	**Må jeg få et kort/en guidebog?**
	mow yie fow eht kawd/ehn guide • bow

TOURIST INFORMATION

Do you have any information on...?	**Har du nogen information om...?**
	hah doo noa • ern in • foh • ma • shoan ohm...
Can you recommend...?	**Kan du anbefale...?**
	kan doo an • beh • fa • ler...

a boat trip	**en bådtur**
	ehn <u>bowdh</u> • toor
an excursion	**en udflugt**
	ehn <u>oodh</u> • floagt
a sightseeing tour	**en rundtur**
	ehn <u>roan</u> • toor

For Asking Directions, see page 65.

(i)

Tourist information offices are located throughout Denmark. The local tourist office can provide a wealth of information on accommodation, activities and other entertainment. An extensive list of all the tourist offices in Denmark can be found on Visit Denmark (www.visitdenmark. com), the Danish Tourist Board's website.

ON TOUR

I'd like to go on the tour to…	**Jeg vil gerne på turen til…**
	yie vil <u>gehr</u> • ner paw <u>too</u> • ern til…
When's the next tour?	**Hvornår starter den næste tur?**
	voar • <u>naw</u> <u>star</u> • dah dehn <u>nehs</u> • der toor
Are there tours in English?	**Er der ture på engelsk?**
	ehr dehr <u>too</u> • ah paw <u>ehng</u> • erlsk
Is there an English-speaking guide/ audio guide?	**Er der en engelsktalende guide/ engelsk lydguide?**
	ehr dehr ehn <u>ehng</u> • erlsk • ta • ler • ner guide/<u>ehng</u> • erlsk <u>lewdh</u> • guide
What time do we leave/return?	**Hvad tid tager vi afsted/kommer vi tilbage?**
	vadh teedh tah vee a • <u>stehdh</u>/<u>koh</u> • mah vee til • <u>ba</u> • yer

We'd like to see...	**Vi vil gerne se...**
	vee vil <u>gehr</u> • ner seh...
Can we stop here...?	**Kan vi stoppe her...?**
	kan vee <u>stoh</u> • ber hehr...
to take	**for at tage billeder**
photographs	*foh ad ta <u>bil</u> • ler • dhah*
to buy souvenirs	**for at købe souvenirs**
	foh ad <u>kur</u> • ber <u>sou</u> • ve • neers
to use the toilets	**for at gå på toilettet**
	foh ad gow paw toa • ee • <u>leh</u> • derdh
Is there access for	**Er der adgang for handicappede?**
the disabled?	*ehr dehr <u>adh</u> • gahng foh*
	<u>han</u> • dee • kah • per • dher

For Tickets, see page 45.

SEEING THE SIGHTS

Where is/are...?	**Hvor er...?**
	voar ehr...
the battleground	**kamppladsen**
	<u>kahmp</u> • plas • sern
the botanical	**den botaniske have**
gardens	*dehn boa • <u>ta</u> • nees • ker <u>ha</u> • ver*
the castle	**slottet**
	<u>sloh</u> • derdh
the downtown	**den indre by**
area	*dehn <u>in</u> • drah bew*
the fountain	**springvandet**
	<u>spring</u> • van • nerdh
the library	**biblioteket**
	beeb • lee • oa • <u>teh</u> • kerdh
the market	**torvet**
	<u>toh</u> • werdh

the museum	**museet**	*moo • say • erdh*
the old town	**den gamle bydel**	*dehn gahm • ler bew • dehl*
the opera house	**Operaen**	*ope • raehn*
the palace	**slottet**	*sloh • derdh*
the park	**parken**	*pah • gern*
the ruins	**ruinerne**	*roo • ee • nah • ner*
the shopping area	**indkøbscentret**	*in • kurbs • sehn • tahdh*
the town square	**rådhuspladsen**	*rawdh • hoos • pla • sern*
Can you show me on the map?	**Kan du vise mig det på kortet?**	*kan doo vee • ser mie deh paw kaw • derdh*
It's…	**Det er…**	*deh ehr…*
amazing	**forbløffende**	*foh • blur • fern • der*
beautiful	**smukt**	*smoakt*
boring	**kedeligt**	*keh • dher • leet*
interesting	**interessant**	*in • trah • sant*
magnificent	**storartet**	*stoar • ah • derdh*
romantic	**romantisk**	*roa • man • tisk*
strange	**underligt**	*oa • nah • leet*

stunning	**fantastisk flot**
	fan • <u>tas</u> • tisk floht
terrible	**frygteligt**
	<u>frurg</u> • ter • leet
ugly	**grimt**
	grimt
I like/don't like it.	**Jeg kan lide/ikke lide det.**
	yie kan lee/<u>ig</u> • ger lee deh

RELIGIOUS SITES

Where's…?	**Hvor er…?**
	voar ehr…
the cathedral	**domkirken**
	<u>dohm</u> • keer • gern
the church	**kirken**
	<u>keer</u> • gern
the mosque	**moskeen**
	moa • <u>skeh</u> • ern
the shrine	**helgengraven**
	<u>hehl</u> • ycrn • gr<u>ah</u> • vern
the synagogue	**synagogen**
	sew • na • <u>goa</u> • ern
the temple	**templet**
	<u>tehmp</u> • lerdh
What time is mass/ the service?	**Hvad tid starter messen/ gudstjenesten?**
	vadh teedh <u>stah</u> • dah
	<u>meh</u> • sern/<u>goodhs</u> • tyeh • ner • stern

ACTIVITIES

SHOPPING

NEED TO KNOW

Where is the market/ mall [shopping centre]?
Hvor ligger markedet/ butikscentret?
voar li • gah mah • ker • dherd/ boo • teeks • sehn • tahdh

I'm just looking.
Jeg ser mig bare omkring.
yie sehr mie bah ohm • kring

Can you help me?
Kan du hjælpe mig?
kan doo yehl • per mie

I'm being helped.
Jeg får hjælp.
yie faw yehlp

How much?
Hvor meget koster det?
voar mie • erdh kohs • dah deh

That's all, thanks.
Det var det hele, tak.
deh vah deh heh • ler tahk

Where do I pay?
Hvor kan jeg betale?
voar kan yie beh • ta • ler

I'll pay in cash/by credit card.
Jeg vil gerne betale kontant/med kreditkort.
yie vil gehr • ner beh • ta • ler kohn • tant/mehdh kreh • deet • kawd

Can I have a receipt?
Kan jeg få en kvittering?
kan yie fow ehn kvee • teh • ring

> (i)
>
> Denmark is an excellent country for shopping. Even in the capital, most shopping can be done on foot. Many of the major international retail stores are located in **Strøget** and **Købmagergade**, Copenhagen´s main pedestrian streets. You can also check out **Vesterbro**, the western part of **Istegade** and the area around **Enghaveplads**. There, you'll find lots of trendy boutiques and pleasant cafes.
>
> For everything under one roof, visit the **Magasin du Nord**, Scandinavia´s largest department store, or the shopping malls: **Field's, Fisketorvet, Frederiksberg Centret** or **Illum**. Regular store hours are Monday to Friday from 9:00 a.m. to 5:30 p.m. On Friday stores are open until as late as 8:00 p.m. and Saturday they are generally open from 10:00 a.m. to 4:00 or 5:00 p.m. Most stores are closed on Sunday.

AT THE SHOPS

Where is…?	**Hvor er…?**
	voar ehr…
the antiques store	**antikvitetshandleren**
	an • tee • kvee • tehts • han • lahn
the bakery	**bageriet**
	ba • yah • ree • erdh
the bank	**banken**
	bahnk • ern
the bookstore	**boghandleren**
	bow • han • lahn
the clothing store	**tøjbutikken**
	toi • boo • tee • gern
the delicatessen	**delikatesseforretningen**
	de • li • ka • tehs • ser • foh • reht • ning • ern

the department store	**stormagasinet**
	stoar • mah • ga • see • nerdh
the gift shop	**gavebutikken**
	_ga_ • ver • boo • tee • gern
the health food store	**helsekostforretningen**
	hehl • ser • kohst • foh • reht • ning • ern
the jeweler	**guldsmeden**
	gool • smeh • dhern
Where is…?	**Hvor er…?**
	voar ehr…
the liquor store [off-licence]	**vinhandelen**
	veen • han • lahn
the market	**markedet**
	mah • ker • dherd
the pastry shop	**konditoriet**
	kohn • dee • toh • _ree_ • erdh
the pharmacy [chemist]	**apoteket**
	ah • poh • _teh_ • kerdh
the produce [grocery] store	**købmanden**
	kur • man • ern
the shoe store	**skoforretningen**
	skoa • foh • reht • ning • ern
the shopping mall [centre]	**butikscentret**
	boo • _teeks_ • sen • trahdh
the souvenir store	**souvenirbutikken**
	soo • veh • _neer_ • boo • tee • kern
the supermarket	**supermarkedet**
	soo • pah • mah • kerdh
the tobacconist	**tobakshandlen**
	toa • _bahks_ • han • lern
the toy store	**legetøjsforretningen**
	lie • er • tois • foh • reht • ning • ern

ASK AN ASSISTANT

When does...open/ close?	**Hvornår åbner/lukker...?** *voar • naw <u>owb</u> • nah/loa • gah...*
Where is...?	**Hvor er...?** *voar ehr...*
the cashier [cash desk]	**kassen** *<u>ka</u> • sern*
the escalator	**rulletrappen** *<u>roo</u> • ler • trah • bern*
the elevator [lift]	**elevatoren** *eh • ler • <u>va</u> • tohn*
the fitting room	**prøverummene** *<u>prur</u> • ver • roa • mer • ner*
the store directory	**butiksoversigten** *boo • <u>teeks</u> • ow • ah • sig • tern*
Can you help me?	**Kan du hjælpe mig?** *kan doo <u>yehl</u> • per mie*
I'm just looking.	**Jeg ser mig bare omkring.** *yie sehr mie bah ohm • <u>kring</u>*
I'm being helped.	**Jeg får hjælp.** *yie faw yehlp*
Do you have any...?	**Har du nogen...?** *hah doo <u>noa</u> • ern...*

Can you show me...? **Kan du vise mig...?**
kan doo <u>vee</u> • ser mie...

Can you ship/ **Kan du forsende det/pakke det ind?**
wrap it? *kan doo foh • <u>seh</u> • ner deh/<u>pah</u> • ger deh in*

How much? **Hvor meget koster det?**
voar <u>mie</u> • erdh <u>kohs</u> • dah deh

That's all, thanks. **Det var det hele, tak.**
deh vah deh <u>heh</u> • ler tahk

For Souvenirs, see page 119.

YOU MAY HEAR...

Kan jeg hjælpe dig?
kan yie <u>yehl</u> • per die

Can I help you?

Lige et øjeblik.
<u>lee</u> • er eht <u>oi</u> • er • blik

One moment.

Hvad skulle det være?
vadj skoo deh <u>vay</u> • er

What would you like?

Skulle der være andet?
skoo dehr <u>vay</u> • er <u>a</u> • nerdh

Anything else?

YOU MAY SEE...

ÅBEN/LUKKET	open/closed
LUKKET FOR FROKOST	closed for lunch
PRØVERUM	fitting room
KASSE	cashier
KUN KONTANTER	cash only
KREDITKORT MODTAGES	credit cards accepted
ÅBNINGSTIDER	business hours
UDGANG	exit

PERSONAL PREFERENCES

I'd like something...	**Jeg vil gerne have noget...**
	yie vil <u>gehr</u> • ner ha <u>noa</u> • erdh...
cheap/expensive	**billigt/dyrt**
	<u>bee</u> • leet/dewrt
larger/smaller	**mindre/større**
	<u>min</u> • drah/<u>stur</u> • ah
from this region	**fra dette område**
	frah <u>deh</u> • ter <u>ohm</u> • row • dher
Is it real?	**Er det ægte?**
	ehr deh <u>ayg</u> • der
Can you show me this/that?	**Kan du vise mig den her/der ?**
	kan doo <u>vee</u> • ser mie dehn hehr/dehr
It's not quite what I want.	**Det er ikke helt det, jeg vil have.**
	deh ehr <u>ig</u> • ger hehlt deh yie vil ha
I don't like it.	**Det bryder jeg mig ikke om.**
	deh <u>brew</u> • dhah yie mie <u>ig</u> • ger ohm
That's too expensive.	**Det er for dyrt.**
	deh ehr foh dewrt
I'd like to think about it.	**Jeg vil gerne tænke lidt over det.**
	yie vil <u>gehr</u> • ner <u>tehn</u> • ger lit <u>oh</u> • wah deh
I'll take it.	**Jeg tager det.**
	yie tah deh

YOU MAY HEAR...

Hvordan ønsker du at betale?	How are
voar • dan urn • skah doo ad beh • ta • ler	you paying?
Dit kreditkort er blevet afvist.	Your credit card
deet kreh • deet • kawd ehr bleh • verdh	has been
aw • vihst	declined.
ID, tak.	ID, please.
ee deh, tahk	
Vi tager ikke mod kreditkort.	We don't accept
vee ta • er ig • ger modh kreh • deet • kawd	credit cards.
Kun kontant, tak.	Cash only,
koon kohn • tant tahk	please.

PAYING & BARGAINING

How much?	**Hvor meget koster det?**
	voar mie • erdh kohs • dah deh
I'll pay...	**Jeg vil gerne betale...**
	yie vil gehr • ner beh • ta • ler...
in cash	**kontant**
	kohn • tant
by credit card	**med kreditkort**
	mehdh kreh • deet • kawd
by traveler's	**med rejsecheck**
cheque	*mehdh rie • ser • shehk*
Can I have	**Kan jeg få en kvittering?**
a receipt?	*kan yie fow ehn kvee • teh • ring*
That's too much.	**Det er for meget.**
	deh ehr foh mie • erdh
I'll give you...	**Jeg kan give dig...**
	yie kan gee die...

I only have…kroner.	**Jeg har kun…kroner.**
	yie hah koon… kroa • nah
Is that your best price?	**Et det den bedste pris, du kan tilbyde mig?**
	ehr deh dehn behs • der prees doo kan til • bew • dher mie
Can you give me a discount?	**Kan jeg få et nedslag i prisen?**
	kan yie fow eht nehdh • sla ee pree • sern

For Numbers, see page 20.

MAKING A COMPLAINT

I'd like…	**Jeg vil gerne…**
	yie vil gehr • ner…
to exchange this	**bytte det her**
	bew • der deh hehr
to return this	**levere det her tilbage**
	leh • veh • ah deh hehr til • ba • yer
a refund	**have mine penge tilbage**
	ha mee • ner pehng • er til • ba • yer
to see the manager	**tale med bestyreren**
	ta • ler mehdh beh • stew • ahn

SERVICES

Can you recommend…?	**Kan du anbefale…?**
	kan doo an • beh • fa • ler…
a barber	**en herrefrisør**
	ehn hehr • er • free • sur
a dry cleaner	**et renseri**
	eht rehn • ser • ree
a hairstylist	**en frisør**
	ehn free • sur

a laundromat [launderette]	**et vaskeri**	*eht vas • ger • <u>ree</u>*
a nail salon	**en neglesalon**	*ehn <u>nie</u> • ler • sa • long*
a spa	**en spa**	*ehn spa*
a travel agency	**et rejsebureau**	*eht <u>rie</u> • ser • bew • roa*
Can you...this?	**Kan du...det her?**	*kan doo...deh hehr*
alter	**ændre**	*<u>ehn</u> • drah*
clean	**rense**	*<u>rehn</u> • ser*
mend	**reparere**	*reh • pah • <u>reh</u> • ah*
press	**presse**	*<u>preh</u> • ser*
When will it be ready?	**Hvornår er det klart?**	*voar • <u>naw</u> ehr deh klahd*

HAIR & BEAUTY

I'd like...	**Jeg vil gerne...**	*yie vil <u>gehr</u> • ner...*
an appointment for today/ tomorrow	**have en tid til i dag/i morgen**	*ha ehn teedh til ee da/ee <u>mohn</u>*
some colour/ highlights	**lidt farver/striber**	*lit fah • vehr/streeh • bher*
my hair styled	**have mit hår sat**	*ha meet haw saht*
a haircut	**klippes**	*<u>kli</u> • pers*

an eyebrow/bikini wax	**en øjenbrynsvoksning/bikinivoksning** *ehn oi • ern • brewns • vohgs • ning/* *bee • kee • nee • vohgs • ning*
a trim	**en studsning** *ehn stuhs • ningh*
a facial	**en ansigtsbehandling** *ehn an • sigts • beh • han • ling*
a manicure/ pedicure	**en manicure/pedicure** *ehn ma • nee • kew • ah/* *peh • dee • kew • ah*
a (sports) massage	**en (sports-)massage** *ehn (spohts)ma • sa • sher*
a trim, please…	**en studsning** *ehn stuhs • ningh*
Don't cut it too short.	**Klip det ikke for kort.** *klip deh ig • ger foh koht*
Shorter here.	**Kortere her.** *koh • dah • rah hehr*
Do you offer…?	**Tilbyder I…?** *tiil • bew • dhah ee…*
acupuncture	**akupunktur** *ah • koo • poank • toor*
aromatherapy	**aromaterapi** *a • roa • ma • teh • rah • pee*

oxygen treatment	**oxygenbehandling**
	ohk • sew • <u>gehn</u> • beh • han • ling
Do you have a sauna?	**Har I en sauna?**
	hah ee ehn <u>sow</u> • na

Many luxury hotels in Denmark offer spa and other health and beauty treatments. Spa resorts and destination spas may be found along the coast throughout Denmark. In recent years the Danish government has instituted rigorous regulations in regard to wellness centers, ensuring a top-quality stay.

ANTIQUES

How old is this?	**Hvor gammelt er det?**
	voar <u>gah</u> • merlt ehr deh
Do you have anything from the...era?	**Har du noget fra...perioden?**
	hah doo <u>noa</u> • erdh fra...
	pehr • ee • <u>oa</u> • dhern
Will I have problems with customs?	**Får jeg problemer i tolden?**
	fow yie proa • bleh • mah ee toh • lern
Does it come with a certificate of authenticity?	**Følger der et ægthedscertifikat med?**
	furl • yah dehr eht
	ehgt • hehdhs • sehr • tee • fee • kat mehdh
Can you ship/ wrap it?	**Kan I sende/pakke det ind?**
	kan ee seh • ner/pah • ker deh in

CLOTHING

I'd like...	**Jeg vil gerne have...**
	yie vil <u>gehr</u> • ner ha...
Can I try this on?	**Må jeg prøve det?**
	mow yie <u>prur</u> • ver deh

It doesn't fit.	**Den passer ikke.**	
	dehn <u>pa</u> • sah <u>ig</u> • ger	
It's too…	**Den er for…**	
	dehn ehr foh…	
big	**stor**	
	stoar	
small	**lille**	
	<u>lee</u> • ler	
short	**kort**	
	<u>kawd</u>	
long	**lang**	
	lahng	
tight	**tæt**	
	tayt	
loose	**løs**	
	lurs	
Do you have this in size…?	**Har du den i størrelse…?**	
	hah doo dehn ee <u>stur</u> • erl • ser…	
Do you have this in a bigger/smaller size?	**Har du den i en større/ mindre størrelse?**	
	hah doo dehn ee ehn <u>stur</u> • ah/<u>min</u> • drah <u>stur</u> • erlser	

For Numbers, see page 20.

YOU MAY HEAR...

Du ser godt ud i den.	That looks great
doo sehr godh oodh ee dehn	on you.
Hvordan passer den?	How does it fit?
voar • dan pah • ser dehn	
Vi har ikke din størrelse.	We don't have
vee hah ig • ger deen stur • rehl • ser	your size.

YOU MAY SEE...

HERRETØJ	men's clothing
DAMETØJ	women's clothing
BØRNETØJ	children's clothing

COLORS

I'd like something...	**Jeg vil gerne have noget...**
	yie vil <u>gehr</u> • ner ha <u>noa</u> • erdh...
gray	**gråt**
	grawht
green	**grønt**
	grurnht
orange	**orange**
	oa • <u>rang</u> • sher
pink	**lyserødt**
	<u>lew</u> • ser • rurdht
purple	**violet**
	vee • oa • <u>leht</u>
red	**rødt**
	rurdht

white	**hvidt**
	veedht
yellow	**gult**
	goolt
beige	**beige**
	baysh
black	**sort**
	soart
blue	**blåt**
	blawht
brown	**brunt**
	broonht

CLOTHES & ACCESSORIES

a backpack	**rygsæk**
	rewg • sehk
a belt	**bælte**
	behl • der
a bikini	**bikini**
	bee • kcc • nee
a blouse	**bluse**
	bloo • ser
a bra	**bh**
	beh • how
underwear	**undertøj**
	oa • nah • tury
panties	**trusser**
	trush • ser
a coat	**frakke**
	frah • ger
a dress	**kjole**
	kyoa • ler
a hat	**hat**
	hat

a jacket	**jakke**
	yah • ger
jeans	**cowboybukser**
	kow • boy • boag • sah
pajamas	**pyjamas**
	pew • _ya_ • mas
pants [trousers]	**bukser**
	boag • sah
panty hose [tights]	**strømpebukser**
	strum • ber • boag • sah
a purse [handbag]	**håndtaske**
	hawn • tas • ger
a raincoat	**regnfrakke**
	rien • frah • ger
a scarf	**tørklæde**
	tur • klay • dher
a shirt	**skjorte**
	skyoar • der
shorts	**shorts**
	sho_h_ts
a skirt	**nederdel**
	neh • dhah • dehl
socks	**sokker**
	soh • gah
stockings	**strømper**
	strum • bah
a suit	**sæt tøj** m /**dragt** f
	seht toi/drahgt
sunglasses	**solbriller**
	soal • bri • lah
a sweater	**sweater**
	sveh • dah
swimming trunks	**badebukser**
	_ba_ • dher • boag • sah

a swimsuit	**badedragt**
	_ba_ • dher • drahgt
a T-shirt	**t-shirt**
	tee • shurd
a tie	**slips**
	slips
underwear	**underbukser**
	_oa_ • nah • boag • sah

FABRIC

I'd like...	**Jeg vil gerne have...**
	yie vil _gehr_ • ner ha...
cotton	**bomuld**
	boh • mool
denim	**denim**
	deh • nim
lace	**blonde**
	blohn • der
leather	**læder**
	lay • dhah
linen	**lærred**
	lehr • erdh

silk	**silke**
	sil • ker
wool	**uld**
	ool
Is it machine washable?	**Kan det maskinvaskes?**
	kan deh ma • <u>skeen</u> • vas • gers

SHOES

I'd like…	**Jeg vil gerne have…**
	yie vil <u>gehr</u> • ner ha…
high-heeled/flat shoes	**et par højhælede/flade sko**
	eht pah <u>hoi</u> • hay • ler • dher/<u>fla</u> • dher skoa
boots	**støvler**
	<u>sturw</u> • lah
loafers	**hyttesko**
	<u>hew</u> • der • skoa
sandals	**sandaler**
	san • <u>da</u> • lah
shoes	**sko**
	skoa
slippers	**hjemmesko**
	<u>yeh</u> • mer • skoa

sneakers	**gummisko**
	goa • mee • skoa
In size...	**I størrelse...**
	ee _stur_ • erl • ser...

SIZES

Small (S)	**lille**
	lee • ler
Medium (M)	**medium**
	meh • dee • oam
Large (L)	**stor**
	stoar
extra large (XL)	**ekstra stor**
	ehk • strah stoar
petite	**petit**
	peh • _teet_
plus size	**ekstra store størrelser**
	ehk • strah stoa • ah _stur_ • erl • sah

NEWSAGENT & TOBACCONIST

Do you sell English-language books/ newspapers?	**Sælger I engelsksprogede bøger/ aviser?**
	sehl • yah ee _ehng_ • erlsk • sprow • er • dher _bur_ • yah/a • _vee_ • sah
I'd like...	**Jeg vil gerne have...**
	yie vil _gehr_ • ner ha...
candy [sweets]	**slik**
	sligh
chewing gum	**tyggegummi**
	tew • ger • gumh • mee
a chocolate bar	**et stykke chokolade**
	ehd stewgh • ger sho • ko • ladher

cigars	**nogle cigarer**
	noa • ler see • gah • ah
a pack/carton	**en pakke/karton cigaretter**
of cigarettes	_ehn pah • ker/kah • tong see • ga • reh • dah_
a lighter	**en lighter**
	ehn lie • dah
a magazine	**et blad**
	eht bladh
matches	**nogle tændstikker**
	noa • ler tehn • sti • gah
a newspaper	**en avis**
	ehn a • vees
a pen	**en pen**
	ehn pehn
a postcard	**et postkort**
	ehd pohst • kawd
a road/town map	**et vejkort/bykort over...**
of...	_eht vie • kawd/bew • kawd oh • wah..._
stamps	**nogle frimærker**
	noa • ler free • mehr • kah

PHOTOGRAPHY

I'd like...camera.	**Jeg vil gerne have...kamera.**
	yie vil gehr • ner ha... ka • meh • rah
an automatic	**et automatisk**
	eht ow • toa • ma • tisk
a digital	**et digitalt**
	eht dee • gee • talt
a disposable	**et engangs-**
	eht ehn • gahngs-
I'd like...	**Jeg vil gerne have...**
	yie vil gehr • ner ha...
a battery	**et batteri**
	eht ba • der • ree

digital prints	**nogle digitaltryk**
	noa • ler dee • gee • _tal_ • trurk
a memory card	**et hukommelseskort**
	eht hoo • _koh_ • merl • sers • kawd
Can I print digital	**Kan jeg udprinte digitale billeder her?**
photos here?	kan yie _oodh_ • prin • der dee • gee • _ta_ • ler
	bil • ler • dhah hehr

SOUVENIRS

aquavit	**akvavit**
	a • kvah • _veet_
amber	**rav**
	rahw
antiques	**antikviteter**
	an • tee • kvee • _teh_ • dah
candles	**stearinlys**
	steh • _reen_ • lews
ceramics	**keramik**
	keh • rah • _meek_
embroidery	**broderi**
	broa • dah • _ree_
furniture	**møbler**
	murb • lah
glassware	**en glasting**
	ehn _glas_ • ting
handmade crafts	**kunsthåndværk**
	koanst • hown • vehrk
knitwear	**strikvarer**
	strik • vah • ah
hand-printed textiles	**håndtrykte tekstilvarer**
	hawn • trurg • der tehk • _steel_ • vah • ah
May I see this/that?	**Må jeg se den/det ?**
	mow yie seh dehn/deh

It's the one in the window/display case.	**Det er den i vinduesudstillingen/ montren.**
	deh ehr dehn ee <u>vin</u>•doos•oodh• stil•ling•ern/<u>mohn</u>•tren
I'd like…	**Jeg vil gerne have…**
	yie vil <u>gehr</u>•ner ha…
a battery	**et batteri**
	eht ba•der•<u>ree</u>
a bracelet	**et armbånd**
	*eht <u>**ahm**</u>•bawn*
a brooch	**en broche**
	ehn <u>broh</u>•sher
earrings	**et par ørenringe**
	eht pah <u>ur</u>•ahn•ring•er
a necklace	**en halskæde**
	*ehn hals•<u>**kay**</u>•dher*
a ring	**en ring**
	ehn ring
a watch	**et ur**
	eht oor
copper	**kobber**
	<u>koh</u>•wah
crystal	**krystal**
	krew•<u>stal</u>
diamonds	**diamanter**
	dee•a•<u>mand</u>
white/yellow gold	**hvidguld/rødguld**
	<u>veedh</u>•gool/<u>rurdh</u>•gool
pearls	**perler**
	<u>pehr</u>•lah
pewter	**tinlegering**
	*tin•leh•<u>**sheh**</u>•ring*
platinum	**platin**
	*pla•<u>**teen**</u>*

sterling silver	**sterlingsølv**
	stehr • ling • surl
Is this real?	**Er det ægte?**
	ehr deh _ehg_ • ter
Can you engrave it?	**Kan du indgravere det?**
	kan doo _in_ • grah • veh • er deh

Denmark is known for its modern design and
quality craftsmanship around the world. You can peruse
the fine silver and jewelry pieces at the **Georg Jensen**
shops in Copenhagen and Århus. **Bang & Olufsen**, known
internationally for its excellent audiovisual equipment, has
shops throughout the country. **Ecco** shoes are easy to find
and **Lego** is available in all toy and department stores.
Holmegård Glas, Stelton, Royal Copenhagen and other
well-known Danish designs can be purchased from interior
design shops as well as department stores. Though your
suitcase might not be big enough, Danes are also famous for
their sleek and practical modern furniture.

SPORT & LEISURE

NEED TO KNOW

When's the game?	**Hvornår starter kampen?** _voar • naw stah • dah kahm • bern_
Where's...?	**Hvor er...?** _voar ehr..._
the beach	**stranden** _strah • nern_
the park	**parken** _pah • gern_
the pool	**svømmebassinet** _svur • mer • ba • sehng • erdh_
Is it safe to swim/ dive here?	**Er det sikkert at svømme/dykke her?** _ehr deh sig • gahd ad svur • mer/ dur • ker hehr_
Can I hire golf clubs?	**Kan jeg leje golfkøller?** _kan yie lie • er gohlf • kur • lah_
How much per hour?	**Hvad koster det per time?** _vadh kohs • dah deh pehr tee • mer_
How far is it to...?	**Hvor langt er der til...?** _voar lahngt ehr dehr til..._
Can you show me on the map?	**Kan du vise mig det på kortet?** _kan doo vee • ser mie deh paw kaw • derdh_

WATCHING SPORT

When's...?	**Hvornår starter...?** _voar • naw stah • dah..._
the baseball game	**baseballkampen** _baseball • kahm • pern_

the basketball game	**basketballkampen** *bah • skerd • bowl • kahm • bern*
the boxing match	**boksekampen** *bohk • ser • kahm • bern*
the cricket game	**cricketkampen** *cricket • kahm • pern*
the cycling race	**cykelløbet** *sew • kerl • lur • berdh*
the golf tournament	**golfturneringen** *gohlf • toor • neh • ing • ern*
the soccer [football] game	**fodboldkampen** *foadh • bohld • kahm • bern*
the tennis match	**tenniskampen** *teh • nees • kahm • bern*
the volleyball game	**volleyballkampen** *voh • lee • bawl • kahm • bern*
Who's playing?	**Hvem spiller?** *vehm speel • lah*
Where's…?	**Hvor er…?** *voar ehr…*
the horsetrack	**hestevæddeløbsbanen** *hehs • der • vay • dher • lurbs • ba • nern*
the racetrack	**væddeløbsbanen** *vay • dher • lurbs • ba • nern*
the stadium	**stadiumet** *sta • dee • oa • merdh*
Where can I place a bet?	**Hvor kan jeg vædde?** *voar kan yie vay • dher*

PLAYING SPORT

Where's…?	**Hvor er…?** *voar ehr…*
the golf course	**golfbanen** *gohlf • ba • nern*

the gym	**motionscentret**
	moa • shoans • cehn • tahdh
the park	**parken**
	pah • gern
the tennis courts	**tennisbanerne**
	ten • nis • ba • nah • ner
How much per...?	**Hvad koster det per...?**
	vadh kohs • dah deh pehr...
day	**dag**
	da
hour	**time**
	tee • mer
game	**spil**
	spil
round	**runde**
	roan • der

Danes are very active people and most of the population participates in regular sporting activities. Sports can mean two things for Danes: **idræt** (an old Scandinavian word for sports) and **sport** (the contemporary term). **Idræt** often refers to the ideas of team-building and well-being associated with playing sports, while **sport** is related to the ideas of performance and athletic achievement.
If you are looking for an active vacation, you can find lots of opportunities for engaging in activities like cycling, sailing, soccer, handball, badminton, horseback riding, fishing and swimming, which are all popular. If you prefer to sit back and watch, sports are regularly broadcast on TV and there are many live events.

Can I hire...?	**Kan jeg leje...?**
	kan yie lie • er...

golf clubs	**golfkøller**
	gohlf • kur • lah
equipment	**udstyr**
	oodh • stewr
a racket	**en ketcher**
	ehn keht • shah

AT THE BEACH/POOL

Where's the beach/pool?	**Hvor ligger stranden/poolen?**
	voar li • gah strah • nern/poo • lern
Is there...?	**Er der...?**
	ehr dehr...
a kiddie [paddling] pool	**et børnebassin**
	eht bur • ner • ba • sehng
an indoor/outdoor pool	**en indendørs/udendørs pool**
	ehn in • ern • durs/oo • dhern • durs pool
a lifeguard	**en livredder**
	ehn leew • ray • dhah
Is it safe...?	**Er det sikkert...?**
	ehr deh si • gaht...
to swim	**at gå i vandet her**
	ad gow ee van • erdh hehr
to dive	**at dykke her**
	ad dur • ker hehr
for children	**for børnene**
	foh bur • ner • ner
I want to hire...	**Jeg vil gerne leje...**
	yie vil gehr • ner lie • er...
a deck chair	**en liggestol**
	ehn lig • ger • stoal
diving equipment	**noget dykkerudstyr**
	eht dur • gah • oodh • stewr
a jet-ski	**nogle jetski**
	noa • ler jeht • skee

Danes are fans of beach vacations and water sports.
There are more than 270 marinas around the country
and all different types of boats and other equipment can be
rented. If you rent a jet-ski or windsurfer, keep in mind that,
in an effort to protect the wildlife, Denmark has very strict
rules regarding where they may be used.

a motorboat	**en motorbåd**
	ehn <u>moa</u> • tah • bowdh
a rowboat	**en robåd**
	ehn <u>roa</u> • bawdh
snorkling	**noget snorkleudstyr**
equipment	*noa • erdh <u>snoh</u> • kler • oodh • stewr*
a surfboard	**et surfbræt**
	eht <u>surf</u> • breht
a towel	**et håndklæde**
	eht <u>hawn</u> • klay • dher
an umbrella	**en parasol**
	ehn pah • rah • <u>sohl</u>
water-skis	**et par vandski**
	eht pah <u>van</u> • skee
a windsurfer	**en windsurfer**
	ehn <u>win</u> • sur • fer
For…hours.	**I…timer.**
	ee…<u>tee</u> • mah

WINTER SPORTS

A lift pass for a day/ **Et liftkort til en dag/fem dage.**
five days, please. *ehd lift • kawd til ehn da/fehm dae*
Where's the ice rink? **Hvor er skøjtebanen.**
voar ehr <u>skoi</u> • der • ba • nern

The mild climate and topography of Denmark are not particularly good for winter sports. However, ice hockey and ice skating are popular.

Are there lessons?	**Tilbyder I undervisning?** *til • bew • dhah ee oa • nah • vees • ning*
How much?	**Hvor meget koster det?** *voar mie • erdh kohs • dah deh*
I'm a beginner.	**Jeg er begynder.** *yie her beh • guw • nah*
I'm experienced.	**Jeg har erfaring.** *yie hah ehr • fahring*
I'd like to rent ice skates.	**Jeg vil gerne leje et par skøjter.** *yie vil gehr • ner lie • er eht pah skoi • dah*
I'd like to hire…	**Jeg vil gerne leje…** *yie vil gehr • ner lie • yer*
boots	**støvler** *sturvl • lah*
a helmet	**en hjelm** *ehn yelm*
poles	**stave** *stah • ve*
skis	**ski** *skih*
a snowboard	**et snowboard** *ehd snowboard*
snowshoes	**snesko** *sneh • skoa*
These are too big/small.	**De er for store/små.** *dee ehr foh stoa • ah/smow*
A trail map, please.	**Et løjpekort.** *ehd lury • peh • kowd*

OUT IN THE COUNTRY

I'd like a map of…	**Jeg vil gerne have et kort over…**
	yie vil gehr•ner ha eht kawd ow•ah…
this region	**dette område**
	deh•deh ohm•row•dher
walking routes	**vandreruter**
	vahn•drah•roo•dah
bike routes	**cykelruter**
	sew•kerl•roo•dah
the trails	**gangstier**
	gahng•stee•ah
Is it easy/difficult?	**Er det nemt/svært?**
	ehr deh nehmt/svehrt
Is it far/steep?	**Er det langt herfra/stejlt?**
	ehr deh lahngt hehr•frah/stielt
How far is it to…?	**Hvor langt er der til…?**
	voar lahngt ehr dehr til…
Can you show me on the map?	**Kan du vise mig det på kortet?**
	kan doo vee•ser mie deh paw kaw•derdh
I'm lost.	**Jeg er faret vild.**
	yie ehr fah•erdh veel
Where's…?	**Hvor er…?**
	voar ehr…
the bridge	**broen**
	broa•ern
the cave	**hulen**
	hoo•lern
the cliff	**klippen**
	kli•bern
the farm	**bondegården**
	boa•ner•gaw•ern
the field	**marken**
	mah•gern

the forest	**skoven**
	skow • ern
the hill	**bakken**
	bah • gern
the lake	**søen**
	sur • ern
the nature	**naturreservatet**
preserve	na • _toor_ • reh • sah • va • derdh
the viewpoint	**udkigsposten**
	oodh • keegs • pohs • dern
the park	**parken**
	pah • gern
the path	**stien**
	stee • ern
the peak	**toppen**
	toph • ern
the picnic area	**picnicområdet**
	pik • nik • ohm • _row_ • dherd
the pond	**dammen**
	dahm • mern
the river	**floden**
	floa • dhern
the sea	**havet**
	_ha_ • verdh

the hot spring	**den varme kilde**
	dehn vah • mern kilh • er
the stream	**åen**
	<u>*ow*</u> *• ern*
the valley	**dalen**
	da • lern
the vineyard	**vingården**
	veen • gaw • ern
the waterfall	**vandfaldet**
	van • falh • ehd

For Asking Directions, see page 65.

TRAVELING WITH CHILDREN

NEED TO KNOW

Is there a discount for kids?	**Er det billigere for børn?**
	ehr deh <u>bee</u> • lee • ah foh burn
Can you recommend a babysitter?	**Kan du anbefale en babysitter?**
	kan doo <u>an</u> • beh • fa • ler ehn
	<u>*bay*</u> *• bee • si • dah*
Can we have a child's seat/ highchair?	**Må vi få et barnesæde/en høj stol?**
	mow vee fow eht <u>bah</u> • ner • say • dher/
	ehn hoi stoal
Where can I change the baby?	**Hvor kan jeg skifte babyen?**
	voar kan yie <u>skeef</u> • der <u>bay</u> • bee • ern

OUT & ABOUT

Can you recommend something for the kids?	**Kan du anbefale noget til børnene?**
	kan doo <u>an</u> • beh • fa • ler <u>noa</u> • erdh til
	<u>*bur*</u> *• ner • ner*

Where's...?	**Hvor er...?**
	voar ehr...
the amusement park	**forlystelsesparken**
	foh • lur • stehl • sers • pah • kern
the arcade	**spillehallen**
	spih • ler • hal • lern
the kiddie [paddling] pool	**børnebassinet**
	bur • ner • ba • sehng • erdh
the park	**parken**
	pah • gern
the playground	**legepladsen**
	lie • er • pla • sern
the zoo	**den zoologiske have**
	dehn soa • loa • gee • sker ha • ver
Are kids allowed?	**Er der adgang for børn?**
	ehr dehr adh • gahng foh burn
Is it safe for kids?	**Er det sikkert for børnene?**
	ehr deh si • gaht foh bur • ner • ner
Is it suitable for... year olds?	**Egner det sig til...årige?**
	ie • nah deh sie til... aw • ree • yer

For Numbers, see page 20.

YOU MAY HEAR...

Hvor er han/hun sød!	How cute he/
voar ehr han/hoon surdh	she is!
Hvad hedder han/hun?	What's his/her
vadh <u>heh</u> • dhah han/hoon	name?
Hvor gammel er han/hun?	How old is he/
voar <u>gah</u> • merl her han/hoon	she?

BABY ESSENTIALS

Do you have...?	**Har du...?**
	har doo...
a baby bottle	**en sutteflaske**
	ehn <u>soo</u> • der • flas • ker
baby food	**babymad**
	bay • bew • madh
baby wipes	**nogen vådservietter**
	<u>noa</u> • ern <u>voadh</u> • sehr • vee • eh • dah
a car seat	**et barnesæde**
	eht <u>bah</u> • ner • say • dher
a children's menu	**en børnemenu**
	ehn <u>bur</u> • ner • meh • new
a children's	**en børneportioner**
portion	*<u>bur</u> • ner • poh • shoa • nah*
a child's seat/	**et barnesæde/en høj stol**
highchair	*eht bah • ner • say • dher/ehn hoi stoal*
a crib	**en barneseng**
	ehn <u>bah</u> • ner • sehng
diapers [nappies]	**nogen bleer**
	<u>noa</u> • ern <u>bleh</u> • ah
formula	**noget mælkeerstatning**
	<u>noa</u> • erdh <u>mehl</u> • ker • ehr • stad • ning

a pacifier [dummy]	**en sut**
	ehn soot
a playpen	**en kravlegård**
	ehn <u>krow</u> • ler • gaw
a stroller	**en klapvogn**
[pushchair]	*ehn <u>klahp</u> • vown*
Can I breastfeed the	**Må jeg amme babyen her?**
baby here?	*mow yie <u>ah</u> • mer bay • bee • ern hehr*
Where can I change	**Hvor kan jeg skifte babyen?**
the baby?	*voar kan yie <u>skeef</u> • der bay • bee • ern*

For Dining with Children, see page 167.

BABYSITTING

Can you recommend	**Kan du anbefale en pålidelig babysitter?**
a reliable babysitter?	*kan doo <u>an</u> • beh • fa • ler ehn*
	paw • <u>lee</u> • dher • lee bay • bee • si • dah
What's the charge?	**Hvad koster det?**
	vadh <u>kohs</u> • dah deh
We'll be back by...	**Vi er tilbage klokken...**
	vee ehr til • <u>ba</u> • yer <u>kloh</u> • gern...
I can be reached	**Jeg kan træffes på...**
at...	*yie kan <u>treh</u> • fers pow...*

HEALTH & SAFETY

EMERGENCIES

NEED TO KNOW		
Help!	**Hjælp!**	
	yehlp	
Go away!	**Gå væk!**	
	gow vehk	
Stop thief!	**Stop tyven!**	
	stohp <u>tew</u> • vern	
Get a doctor!	**Tilkald læge!**	
	til • kal <u>lay</u> • er	
Fire!	**Det brænder!**	
	deh <u>brahn</u> • <u>nah</u>	
I'm lost.	**Jeg er faret vild**	
	yie ehr <u>fah</u> • erdh veel	
Can you help me?	**Kan du hjælpe mig?**	
	kan doo <u>yehl</u> • per mie	

POLICE

NEED TO KNOW

Call the police!	**Ring til politiet!**
	ring til poa • lee • tee • erdh
Where's the police station?	**Hvor ligger politistationen?**
	voar li • gah
	poa • lee • tee • sta • shoa • nern
There has been an accident/attack.	**Der er sket en ulykke/et overfald.**
	dehr ehr skeht ehn oo • lur • ker/
	eht ow • ah • fal
My child is missing.	**Mit barn er blevet væk.**
	meet bahn ehr bleh • erdh vehk
I need...	**Jeg har brug for...**
	yie hah broo foh...
an interpreter	**en tolk**
	ehn tohlk
to contact my lawyer	**at tale med min advokat**
	ad ta • ler mehdh meen adh • voa • kat
to make a phone call	**at lave en opringning**
	ad la • ver ehn ohb • ring • ning
I'm innocent.	**Jeg er uskyldig.**
	yie ehr oo • skewl • dee

CRIME & LOST PROPERTY

I want to report...	**Jeg vil anmelde...**
	yie vil an • meh • ler...
a mugging	**et overfald**
	eht ow • ah • fal
a rape	**en voldtægt**
	ehn vohl • tehkt
a theft	**et tyveri**
	eht tew • ah • ree

YOU MAY HEAR...

Udfyld venligst denne formular.	Fill out this
oodh • fewl <u>vehn</u> • leest <u>deh</u> • neh foh • moo • <u>lah</u>	form.
Vis venligst dit ID.	Your ID, please.
vees vehn • leesd deet ee deh	
Hvornår/Hvor skete det?	When/Where did
voar • <u>naw</u>/voar <u>skeh</u> • der deh	it happen?
Hvordan ser han/hun ud?	What does
voar • <u>dan</u> sehr han/hoon oodh	he/she look like?

I've been robbed/ mugged	**Jeg er blevet bestjålet/overfaldet.**
	yie ehr <u>bleh</u> • erdh beh • <u>styow</u> • lerdh/ <u>ow</u> • ah • fa • lerdh
I've lost...	**Jeg har tabt...**
	yie hah tahbt
...has been stolen.	**...er blevet stjålet.**
	...ehr <u>bleh</u> • erdh <u>styow</u> • lerdh
My backpack	**Min rygsæk**
	meen <u>rewg</u> • sehk
My bicycle	**Min cykel**
	meen <u>sew</u> • gel
My camera	**Mit kamera**
	meet <u>ka</u> • meh • rah
My (rental) car	**Min (lejede) bil**
	meen (<u>lie</u> • er • dher) beel
My computer	**Min pc**
	meen peh • seh
My credit cards	**Mit kreditkort**
	meet kreh • <u>deet</u> • kawd

My jewelry	**Mine smykker**
	mee • ner <u>smur</u> • kah
My money	**Mine penge**
	mee • ner <u>pehng</u> • er
My passport	**Mit pas**
	meet pas
My purse [handbag]	**Min håndtaske**
	meen <u>hawn</u> • tas • ger
...has been stolen.	**...er blevet stjålet.**
	...ehr <u>bleh</u> • erdh sty<u>ow</u> • lerdh
My traveler's cheques	**Mine rejsechecks**
	mee • ner <u>rie</u> • ser • shehk
My wallet	**Min tegnebog**
	meen <u>tie</u> • ner • bow
I need a police report for my insurance.	**Jeg skal bruge en politianmeldelse til min forsikring.**
	yie skal <u>broo</u> • er ehn poa • lee • <u>tee</u> • an • meh • lerl • ser til meen foh • <u>sik</u> • ring
Where is the British/American/Irish embassy?	**Hvor er den den engelske/amerikanske/irske ambassade?**
	voar ehr dehn <u>en</u> • ghel • sger/ <u>ama</u> • ree • kansger/ir • sger <u>amh</u> • bah • sa • dher

HEALTH

NEED TO KNOW

I'm sick [ill].	**Jeg er syg.** *yie ehr sew*
I need an English-speaking doctor.	**Jeg har brug for en læge, der taler engelsk.** *yie hah broo foh ehn <u>lay</u>•er dehr ta•lah <u>ehng</u>•erlsk*
It hurts here.	**Det gør ondt her.** *deh gur ohnt hehr*
I have a stomachache.	**Jeg har mavepine.** *yie hah <u>ma</u>•ver•**pee**•ner*

FINDING A DOCTOR

Can you recommend a doctor/dentist?	**Kan du anbefale en læge/tandlæge?** *kan doo <u>an</u>•beh•**fa**•ler ehn <u>lay</u>•er/<u>tan</u>•**lay**•er*

Can the doctor come to see me here?	**Kunne lægen komme for at se mig her?**
	koo • ner lay • ern koh • mer foh ad seh mie hehr
I need an English-speaking doctor.	**Jeg har brug for en læge, der taler engelsk.**
	yie hah broo foh ehn lay • er dehr ta • lah ehng • erlsk
What are the office hours?	**Hvornår er der åbent?**
	voar • naw ehr dehr ow • bernt
Can I make an appointment...?	**Kan jeg få en tid...?**
	kan yie fow ehn teedh...
for today	**i dag**
	_ee da_
for tomorrow	**i morgen**
	ee mohn
as soon as possible	**så snart som muligt**
	saw snaht sohm moo • leet
It's urgent.	**Det haster.**
	deh has • dah

SYMPTOMS

I'm...	**Jeg...**
	yie...
bleeding	**bløder**
	blur • dhah
constipated	**er forstoppet**
	ehr foh • stoh • berdh
dizzy	**er svimmel**
	ehr svim • merl
nauseous	**har kvalme**
	hah kval • mer
vomiting	**har kastet op**
	hah kas • derdh ohb

It hurts here.	**Det gør ondt her.** *deh gur ohnt hehr*
I have...	**Jeg har...** *yie hah...*
an allergic reaction	**en allergisk reaktion** *ehn a • lehr • geesk reh • ahk • shoan*
chest pain	**brystsmerter** *brurst • smehr • dah*
cramps	**kramper** *krahm • bar*
diarrhea	**diarré** *dia • rah*
an earache	**ondt i ørerne** *ohnt ee ur • ah • ner*
a fever	**feber** *feh • bah*
pain	**smerter** *smehr • dah*
a rash	**fået udslet** *fow • erdh oodh • sleht*
a sprain	**en forstuvning** *ehn for • stuw • ning*

some swelling	**fået en hævelse**
	fow•erdh ehn _hay_•vel•ser
a stomachache	**mavepine**
	_ma_•ver•_pee_•ner
sunstroke	**solstik**
	soal•stik
I've been sick for...days.	**Jeg har været syg i...dage.**
	yie hah _vay_•erdh sew ee... _da_•e

For Numbers, see page 20.

CONDITIONS

I'm...	**Jeg har...**
	yie hah...
anemic	**blodmangel**
	bloadh•mahng•erl
asthmatic	**astma**
	ast•ma
diabetic	**sukkersyge**
	soa•gah•_sew_•er
I'm epileptic.	**Jeg er epileptiker.**
	yie ehr epi•_lehp_•tiger
I'm allergic to antibiotics/ penicillin.	**Jeg er allergisk over for antibiotika/ pencilin.**
	yie ehr a•_lehr_•geesk _ow_•ah•foh an•tee•bee•_oa_•tee•ka/ pehn•see•_leen_
I have arthritis/ (high/low) blood pressure.	**Jeg har gigt/(højt/lavt) blodtryk.**
	yie hah geegt/(hoit/lavt) _bloadh_•trurk
I'm on...	**Jeg tager...**
	yie t**ah**...
I have a heart condition.	**Jeg har en hjertesygdom.**
	yie hah ehn _yehr_•der•_sew_•dohm

For Dietary Requirements, see page 165.

YOU MAY HEAR...

Hvad er der galt?	What's wrong?
vadh ehr dehr galt	
Hvor gør det ondt?	Where does it
voar gur deh ohnt	hurt?
Gør det ondt her?	Does it hurt
gur deh ohnt hehr	here?
Tager du nogen anden medicin?	Are you taking
tah doo noa•ern a•nern	any other
meh•dee•seen	medication?
Er du allergisk over for noget?	Are you allergic
ehr doo a•lehr•geesk ow•ah•foh	to anything?
noa•erdh	
Luk munden op.	Open your
loak moa•nern ohb	mouth.
Tag en dyb indånding.	Breathe deeply.
ta ehn dewb in•own•ning	
Vær venlig at hoste.	Cough, please.
vehr vehn•lee ad hohs•der	
Du skal indlægges på hospitalet til	I want you to go
undersøgelse.	to the hospital.
doo skal in•lay•gers paw	
hoa•spee•ta•lerdh til	
oa•nah•sur•yerl•ser	

TREATMENT

Do I need
a prescription/
medicine?

Skal jeg have en recept/medicin?
skal yie hah ehn reh•cebt/meh•di•cin

Can you prescribe a generic drug [unbranded medication]?	**Kan du udskrive den billigste medicin?** *kan doo oodh • skriwe dehn* *bee • lees • der meh • di • cin*
Where can I get it?	**Hvor kan jeg få det?** *voar kan yie fow deh*

For Pharmacy, see page 148.

HOSPITAL

Please notify my family.	**Vær venlig og underret min familie.** *vehr vehn • lee ow oa • nah • reht meen* *fa • meel • yer*
I'm in pain.	**Jeg har smerter.** *yie hah smehr • dah*
I need a doctor/ nurse.	**Jeg har brug for en læge/sygeplejerske.** *yie hah broo foh ehn lay • er/* *sew • er • plie • ah • sker*
When are visiting hours?	**Hvornår er der besøgstid?** *voar • naw ehr dehr beh • surs • teedh*
I'm visiting...	**Jeg er her for at besøge...** *yie ehr hehr foh ad beh • sur • yer...*

DENTIST

I've broken a tooth/ lost a filling.	**Jeg har brækket en tand/tabt en plombe.** *yie hah bray • gerdh ehn tan/tabt ehn* *ploam • ber*
I have a toothache.	**Jeg har tandpine.** *yie hah tan • pee • ner*
Can you fix this denture?	**Kan du reparere min protese?** *kan doo reh • pah • reh • ah meen* *proa • teh • ser*

GYNECOLOGIST

I have menstrual cramps/a vaginal infection.	**Jeg har menstruationssmerter/ underlivsbetændelse.** *yie hah mehn • stroo • a shoans • smehr • dah/oa • nah • lee vs • beh • teh • nel • ser*
I missed my period.	**Jeg har ikke fået min menstruation.** *yie hah ig • ger fow • erdh meen mehn • stroo • a • shoan*
I'm on the Pill.	**Jeg tager p-piller.** *yie tah p eh • pil • lah*
I'm (...months) pregnant.	**Jeg er (...måneder) henne.** *yie ehr (...maw • nedh • ar) heh • ner*
I'm (not) pregnant.	**Jeg er (ikke) gravid.** *yie ehr (ig • ger) grah • veedh*
I haven't had my period for...months.	**Jeg har ikke haft menstruation i... måneder.** *yie hah ig • ger hahft mehn • stroo • a • shoan ee... mow • ner • dhah*

For Numbers, see page 20.

OPTICIAN

I've lost...	**Jeg har tabt....** *yie hah tahbt...*
a contact lens	**en af mine kontaktlinser** *ehn a mee • ner kohn • tahkt • lin • sah*
my glasses	**mine briller** *mee • ner bril • lah*
a lens	**en kontaktlinse** *ehn kohn • tahkt • lin • ser*

PAYMENT & INSURANCE

How much? **Hvor meget koster det?**
voar <u>mie</u> • erdh <u>kohs</u> • dah deh

Can I pay by credit card? **Kan jeg betale med kreditkort?**
kan yie beh • <u>ta</u> • ler mehdh kreh • <u>deet</u> • kawd

I have insurance. **Jeg er forsikret.**
yie ehr foh • <u>sik</u> • rerdh

Can I have a receipt for my insurance? **Må jeg få en kvittering til min sygeforsikring?**
mow yie fow ehn kvee • <u>teh</u> • ring til meen <u>sew</u> • er • foh • sik • ring

For Money, see page 30.

PHARMACY

NEED TO KNOW

Where's the nearest pharmacy?
Hvor er det nærmeste apotek?
voar ehr deh nehr•meh•ster ah•poa•tehk

What time does the pharmacy open/close?
Hvornår åbner/lukker apoteket?
voar•naw ow b•nah/loa•gah ah•poa•teh•kerdh

What would you recommend for...?
Hvad ville du anbefale mod...?
vadh vee•ler doo an•beh•fa•ler moadh...

Can you fill [make up] this prescription for me?
Kan du give mig, hvad der står på recepten?
kan doo gee mie vadh dehr staw pow reh•sehp•dern

I'm allergic to...
Jeg er allergisk over for...
yie her a•lehr•geesk ow•ah foh...

In Denmark, an **apotek** (pharmacy) fills medical prescriptions, while a **parfumeri** sells non-prescription items, such as toiletries and cosmetics. Regular hours are Monday to Thursday from 9:00 a.m. to 5:30 p.m. Pharmacies may close at 7:00 p.m. on Fridays and 1:00 p.m. on Saturdays. At other times, they work on a rotating schedule. Check the store window to find the closest pharmacy open.

WHAT TO TAKE

YOU MAY SEE...	👁
EN GANG/TRE GANGE DAGLIGT	once/three times a day
PILLER	tablets
DRÅBER	drops
TESKEER	teaspoons
FØR/EFTER/I FORBINDELSE	before/after
MED ET MÅLTID	with meals
PÅ TOM MAVE	on an empty stomach
SLUG DEM HELE	swallow whole
KAN VIRKE DØSENDE	may cause drowsiness
KUN TIL UDVORTES BRUG	for external use only

How much should I take?
Hvor meget skal jeg tage?
voar mie • erdh skal yie ta

How often?
Hvor ofte?
voar ohf • der

Is it suitable for children?
Egner det sig til børn?
ie • nah deh sie til burn

I'm taking...
Jeg tager...
yie tah...

Are there side effects?
Er der nogen bivirkninger?
ehr dehr noa • ern bee • veerk • ning • ah

I'd like some medicine for...
Jeg vil gerne have noget mod...
yie vil gehr • ner ha noa • erdh moadh...

  a cold
  forkølelse
  foh • kur • lerl • ser

  a cough
  hoste
  hoa • ster

diarrhea	**diarré**
	dee • a • <u>reh</u>
a headache	**hovedpine**
	hoh • ed • peeh • ner
insect bites	**insektbid**
	in • segt • beedh
motion sickness	**køresyge**
	<u>kur</u> • ah • sew • er
a sore throat	**øm hals**
	urm hals
sunburn	**solforbrænding**
	<u>soal</u> • foh • breh • ning
a toothache	**tandpine**
	tan • peeh • ner
an upset stomach	**dårlig mave**
	<u>daw</u> • lee <u>ma</u> • ver

BASIC SUPPLIES

I'd like...	**Jeg vil gerne have...**
	yie vil <u>gehr</u> • ner ha...
acetaminophen	**en æske paracetamol**
[paracetamol]	*ehn <u>ehs</u> • ker pah • rah • seh • ta • <u>moal</u>*

antiseptic cream	**en antiseptisk creme**
	ehn <u>an</u> • tee • sehp • tisk krehm
aspirin	**en æske hovedpinepiller**
	ehn <u>ehs</u> • ger <u>ho</u> • wed • pee • ner • pil • lah
bandages	**noget plaster**
[plasters]	*<u>noa</u> • erdh <u>plas</u> • dah*
a comb	**en kam**
	ehn kahm
condoms	**nogle kondomer**
	<u>noa</u> • ler kohn • <u>doa</u> • mah
contact lens	**noget kontaküinsevæske**
solution	*<u>noa</u> • erdh kohn • <u>tahkt</u> • lin • ser • vehs • ger*
deodorant	**deodorant**
	deh • oa • doa • <u>rahnt</u>
a hairbrush	**en hårbørste**
	ehn haw • burr • sder
hairspray	**noget hårlak**
	<u>noa</u> • erdh <u>haw</u> • lahk
ibuprofen	**en æske ibuprofen**
	ehn <u>ehs</u> • ger ee • boo • proa • fehn
insect repellent	**en insekt-spray**
	ehn in • <u>sehkt</u> • spray
a nail file	**en neglefil**
	ehn <u>nie</u> • ler • feel

a (disposable) razor	**en barberskraber**
	ehn bah • behr • skrah • bah
razor blades	**nogle barberblade**
	noa • ler bah • behr • bla • dher
sanitary napkins [towels]	**nogle hygiejnebind**
	noa • ler hew • gee • ie • ner • bin
shampoo/ conditioner	**noget shampoo/hårbalsam**
	noa • erdh shahm • poa/haw • bal • sahm
soap	**et stykke sæbe**
	eht stur • ger say • ber
sunscreen	**noget solcreme**
	noa • erdh soal • krehm
tampons	**nogle tamponer**
	noa • ler tahm • pong • ah
tissues	**nogle papirlommetørklæder**
	noa • ler pah • peer • loh • mer • tur • kl ay • dhah
toilet paper	**noget toiletpapir**
	noa • erdh toa • ee • leht • pah • peer
I'd like...	**Jeg vil gerne have...**
	yie vil gehr • ner ha...
a toothbrush	**en tandbørste**
	ehn tahn • bur • ster

toothpaste **noget tandpasta**
noa • erdh _tahn_ • pas • ta

For Baby Essentials, see page 132.

CHILD HEALTH & EMERGENCY

Can you recommend **Kan du anbefale en børnelæge?**
a pediatrician? kan doo <u>an</u> • beh • **fa** • ler ehn
<u>bur</u> • ner • **lay** • er

My child is allergic **Mit barn er allergisk overfor...**
to... meet b**ah**n ehr a • <u>lehr</u> • gisk <u>ow</u> • ah • foh...

My child is missing. **Mit barn er blevet væk.**
meet b**ah**n ehr <u>bleh</u> • werdh vehk

Have you seen a **Har du set en dreng/pige?**
boy/girl? hah doo seht ehn drehng/<u>pee</u> • er

For Police, see page 137.

DISABLED TRAVELERS

NEED TO KNOW

Is there...?	**Er der...?**
	ehr dehr...
access for the disabled	**adgang for handicappede**
	<u>adh</u> • gahng for <u>han</u> • dee • kahp • per • dher
a wheelchair ramp	**en rampe til kørestole**
	ehn <u>rahm</u> • ber tilkur • ah • st<u>oa</u> • ler
a disabled-accessible toilet	**et handicaptoilet**
	eht <u>han</u> • dee • kahp • toa • ee • lehd
I need...	**Jeg har brug for...**
	yie hah br<u>oo</u> foh...
assistance	**hjælp**
	yehlp
an elevator [lift]	**en elevator**
	ehn eh • ler • <u>va</u> • toh
a ground-floor room	**et værelse i stueetagen**
	eht <u>vehrl</u> • ser ee st<u>oo</u> • er • eh • ta • shern

ASKING FOR ASSISTANCE

I'm disabled.	**Jeg er handicappet.**
	yie ehr<u>han</u> • dee • kah • perdh
I'm deaf.	**Jeg er døv.**
	yie ehr durv

I'm visually/hearing impaired.	**Jeg er synshæmmet/hørehæmmet.**
	yie ehr <u>sewns</u>•heh•merdh/
	<u>hur</u>•ah•hehm•merdh
I'm unable to walk far/use the stairs.	**Jeg kan ikke gå langt/op ad trapperne.**
	yie kan <u>ig</u>•ger gow lahngt/ohb a
	<u>trah</u>•bah•ner
Can I bring my wheelchair?	**Må jeg tage min kørestol med?**
	*mow yie ta meen <u>kur</u>•ah•sto**al** mehdh*
Are guide dogs permitted?	**Er der adgang for førerhunde?**
	ehr dehr <u>adh</u>•gahng foh <u>fur</u>•ah•hoo•ner
Can you help me?	**Kan du hjælpe mig?**
	kan doo <u>yehl</u>•per mie
Please open/hold the door.	**Åbn/Hold venligst døren.**
	owbn/hohl <u>vehn</u>•leest <u>dur</u>•ern

For Emergencies, see page 136.

FOOD & DRINK

EATING OUT

NEED TO KNOW

Can you recommend a good restaurant/ bar?	**Kan du anbefale en god restaurant/ bar?** *kan doo <u>an</u> • <u>beh</u> • <u>fa</u> • <u>ler</u> ehn <u>goadh</u> reh • stoa • <u>rang</u>/b<u>ah</u>*
Is there a traditional Danish/ an inexpensive restaurant nearby?	**Ligger der en typisk dansk/ikke så dyr restaurant i nærheden?** *<u>li</u> • gah dah ehn <u>tew</u> • peesk dansk/ <u>ig</u> • ger saw dewr reh • stoa • rang ee nehr • <u>heh</u> • dhern*
A table for..., please.	**Et bord til...tak.** *eht boar til...tahk*
Can we sit...?	**Må vi sidde...?** *mow vee si • dher...*
here/there	**her/der** *hehr/dehr*
outside	**udenfor** *oo • dhern • foh*
at a non-smoking table	**ved et bord for ikke-rygere** *vehdh eht boar foh ig • ger • rew • ah*
I'm waiting for someone.	**Jeg venter på nogen.** *yie vehn • dah paw noa • ern*
Where are the toilets?	**Hvor er toilettet?** *voar her toa • ee • leh • derdh*
I'd like a menu, please.	**Jeg vil gerne bede om et menukort, tak.** *yie vil gehr • ner beh ohm eht meh • new • kawd tahk*

What do you recommend?	**Hvad kan du anbefale?**
	vadh kan doo an • beh • fa • ler
I'd like…	**Jeg vil gerne have…**
	yie vil gehr • ner ha…
Some more, please.	**Jeg vil gerne have lidt mere, tak.**
	*yie vil gehr • ner ha lit m**eh** • ah tahk*
Enjoy your meal.	**Velbekomme.**
	vehl • beh • koh • mer
Can I have the check [bill]?	**Kan jeg få regningen?**
	kan yie fow rie • ning • ern
Is service included?	**Er drikkepenge inkluderet?**
	*ehr drig • ger • pehng • er in • kloo • **deh** • rerdh*
Can I pay by credit card?	**Kan jeg betale med kreditkort?**
	*kan yie beh • **ta** • ler mehdh kreh • deet • kawd*
Can I have a receipt?	**Kan jeg få en kvittering?**
	*kan yie fow ehn kvee • **teh** • ring*
Thank you.	**Tak.**
	tahk

WHERE TO EAT

Can you recommend…?	**Kan du anbefale…?**
	kan dooan • beh • fa • ler…
a restaurant	**en restaurant**
	ehn reh • stoa • rang
a bar	**en bar**
	*ehn b**ah***
a cafe	**en café**
	*ehn ca • f**eh***

a fast-food place	**en burgerbar**
	ehn bur•gah•bah
a cheap restaurant	**en billig restaurant**
	ehn bee•lee res•taw•rangh
an expensive restaurant	**en dyr restaurant**
	ehn dewr res•taw•rangh
a restaurant with a good view	**en restaurant med god udsigt**
	ehn res•taw•rangh medh gohd oodh•sight
an authentic/ a non-touristy restaurant	**en autentisk/ikke-turistet restaurant**
	ehn aw•ten•tisk/ig•ger tuh•rist•ehd res•taw•rangh

RESERVATIONS & PREFERENCES

I'd like to reserve a table...	**Jeg vil gerne bestille et bord...**
	yie vil gehr•ner beh•stil•ler eht boar...
for two	**til to**
	til toa
for this evening	**til i aften**
	til ee ahf•tern
for tomorrow at...	**til i morgen klokken...**
	til ee mawn kloh•gehrn...
A table for two, please.	**Et bord til to, tak.**
	eht boar til toa tahk
We have a reservation.	**Vi har en reservation.**
	vee hah ehn reh•sah•va•shoan
My name is...	**Mit navn er...**
	meet nown ehr...
Can we sit...?	**Må vi sidde...?**
	mow vee si•dher...
here/there	**her/der**
	hehr/dehr
outside	**udenfor**
	oo•dhern•foh

YOU MAY HEAR...

Har du bestilt et bord?
hah doo beh • stild eht boar

Til hvor mange?
til voar mang • er

Ryger eller ikke • ryger?
rew • ah ehl • lah ig • ger rew • ah

Er I klar til at bestille?
ehr ee klah til ad beh • stil • ler

Hvad kunne I tænke jer?
vadh koo • ner ee tehn • ker yehr

Jeg kan anbefale...
yie kan an • beh • fa • ler....

Velbekomme.
vehl • beh • koh • mer

Do you have
a reservation?

For how many?

Smoking or non-
smoking?

Are you ready to
order?

What would you
like?

I recommend...

Enjoy your meal.

at a non-smoking table	**ved et bord for ikkerygere** *vehdh eht boar for ig • ger • rew • ah*
by the window	**ved vinduet** *vehdh vin • doo • erdh*

in the shade	**i skyggen**
	ee skewg • gehn
in the sun	**i solen**
	ee sohl • ehn
Where are the toilets?	**Hvor er toilettet?**
	voar ehr toa • ee • leh • derdh

> ⓘ
>
> **Moms** (sales tax or value-added tax) and service charges are already included in your final bill in restaurants. Tips for outstanding service are a matter of personal choice.

HOW TO ORDER

Waiter/Waitress!	**Tjener/Frøken!**
	*ty**eh** • nah/frur • kern*
We're ready to order.	**Vi er klar til bestille.**
	vee ehr klah til ad beh • stil • ler
May I see the wine list?	**Må jeg bede om en vinliste?**
	*mow yie beh ohm ehn v**ee**n • lis • der*
I'd like...	**Jeg vil gerne have...**
	yie vil gehr • ner ha...
a bottle of...	**en flaske...**
	ehn flas • ger...
a carafe of...	**en karaffel...**
	*ehn ka • **rah** • ferl...*
a glass of...	**et glas...**
	eht glas...
Can I have a menu?	**Må jeg bede om et menukort?**
	mow yie beh ohm eht meh • new • kawd
Do you have...?	**Er der...?**
	ehr dehr...

a menu in English	**et menukort på engelsk**
	eht meh • new • kawd paw ehng • erlsk
a fixed price menu	**et dagens tilbud**
	eht d<u>a</u> • erns til • boodh
a children's menu	**en børnemenu**
	ehn bur • ner • meh • new
What do you recommend?	**Hvad kan du anbefale?**
	vadh kan doo an • beh • fa • ler
What's this?	**Hvad er det?**
	vadh ehr deh
What's in it?	**Hvad er der i?**
	vadh ehr da ee
Is it spicy?	**Er det krydret?**
	ehr deh krewdh • rerdh
I'd like...	**Jeg vil gerne have...**
	yie vil gehr • ner ha...
More...please.	**Mere...tak.**
	m<u>eh</u> • ah...tahk
With/Without...	**Med/Uden...**
	mehdh/<u>oo</u> • dhern...
I can't eat...	**Jeg må ikke spise...**
	yie mow ig • ger spee • ser...

rare	**letstegt**
	leht • stehgt
medium	**medium**
	*m**eh** • dee • oam*
well done	**gennemstegt**
	geh • nerm • stehgt
It's to go	**Jeg tager det med mig.**
[take away].	*yie tah deh mehdhmie*

For Drinks, see page 194.

COOKING METHODS

baked	**bagt**
	bahgt
boiled	**kogt**
	kohgt
braised	**grydestest**
	*gr**ew** • dher • stehgt*
breaded	**paneret**
	*pa • n**eh** • rerdh*
creamed	**tilberedt med fløde**
	*til • beh • rehd mehdh fl**ur** • dher*

diced	**skåret i terninger**
	skaw • rerdh ee tehr • ning • ah
fileted	**fileteret**
	fee • leh • teh • rerdh
fried	**stegt**
	stehgt
grilled	**grillet**
	gree • lerdh
poached	**pocheret**
	poa • sheh • rerdh
roasted	**ovnstegt**
	own • stehgt
sautéed	**sauteret**
	saw • teh • rerdh
smoked	**røget**
	roi • erdh
steamed	**dampet**
	dahm • berdh
stewed	**stuvet**
	stoo • erdh
stuffed	**farseret**
	fah • seh • rerdh

DIETARY REQUIREMENTS

I'm...	**Jeg...**
	yie…
diabetic	**har sukkersyge**
	hah soa • gah • sew • er
lactose intolerant	**er laktoseallergiker**
	ehr lahk • toa • ser • a • lehr • gee • gar
vegetarian	**er vegetar**
	ehr veh • geh • tah
vegan	**veganer**
	veh • gah • nehr

I'm allergic to...	**Jeg kan ikke tåle...**
	yie kan ig • ger t__ow__ • ler...
I can't eat...	**Jeg kan ikke spise...**
	yie kan ig • ger sp__ee__ ser...
dairy	**mælkeprodukter**
	mehl • ker • proa • doag • dah
gluten	**gluten**
	gl__oo__ • dern
nuts	**nødder**
	nur • dhah
pork	**svinekød**
	sv__ee__ • ner • kurdh
shellfish	**skaldyr**
	skal • dewr
spicy foods	**krydret mad**
	kr__ew__dh • rerdh madh
wheat	**hvede**
	v__eh__ • dher
Is it halal/kosher?	**Er det halal/kosher?**
	ehr deh ha • lal/koh • sher
Do you have...?	**Har I...?**
	hah ee...
skimmed milk	**skummetmælk**
	skum • medh • mehlk

whole milk	**sødmælk**
	surdh • mehlk
soya milk	**soyamælk**
	soya • mehlk

DINING WITH CHILDREN

Do you have children's portions?	**Serverer I mad i børneportioner?**
	sehr • veh • ah ee madh ee bur • ner • poh • shoa • nah
A highchair/child's seat, please.	**Jeg vil gerne bede om en høj stol/et barnesæde, tak.**
	yie vil gehr • ner beh ohm ehn hoi stoal/eht bah • ner • say • dher tahk
Where can I feed/ change the baby?	**Hvor kan jeg made/skifte babyen?**
	voar kan yie ma • dher/skeef • der bay • bee • ern
Can you warm this?	**Kan du opvarme dette?**
	kan doo ohb • vah • mer deh • deh

For Traveling with Children, see page 130.

HOW TO COMPLAIN

How much longer will our food be?	**Hvor lang tid tager det, før maden er klar?**
	voar lahng teedh tah deh fur ma • dhern ehr klah
We can't wait any longer.	**Vi kan ikke vente længere.**
	vee kan ig • ger vehn • der layng • ah
We're leaving.	**Vi går.**
	vee gaw
I didn't order this.	**Det har jeg ikke bestilt.**
	deh hah yie ig • ger beh • stilt

I ordered…	**Jeg bad om…**
	yie badh ohm…
I can't eat this.	**Jeg kan ikke spise det her.**
	yie kan ig•ger spee•ser deh hehr
This is too…	**Det her er for…**
	deh hehr ehr foh…
cold/hot	**koldt/varmt**
	kohlt/vahmt
salty/spicy	**saltet/krydret**
	sal•terdh/krewdh•rerdh
tough/bland	**sejt/har ingen smag**
	sied/hahing•ern sma
This isn't clean/	**Det her er ikke rent/frisk.**
fresh.	*deh hehr ehr ig•ger rehnt/frisk*

PAYING

I'd like the check	**Må jeg bede om regningen.**
[bill].	*mow yie beh ohm rie•ning•ern*
We'd like to pay	**Vi vil gerne betale hver for sig.**
separately.	*vee vil gehr•ner beh•ta•ler vehr foh sie*
It's all together.	**Vi vil gerne betale samlet.**
	vee vil gehr•ner beh•ta•ler sahm•lerdh
Is service included?	**Er drikkepenge inkluderet?**
	ehr drig•ger•pehng•er
	in•kloo•deh•erdh
What's this	**Hvad dækker dette beløb?**
amount for?	*vadh day•gah deh•der beh•lurb*
I didn't have that..	**Det har jeg ikke bestilt. Jeg fik…**
I had…	*deh hah yie ig•ger beh•stilt yie feek…*
Can I pay by credit	**Kan jeg betale med kreditkort?**
card?	*kan yie beh•ta•ler mehdh*
	kreh•deet•kawd

| Can I have an itemized bill/a receipt ? | **Må jeg bede om en udspecificeret regning/en kvittering?** *mow yie beh ohm ehn oodh • speh • see • fee • seh • ahdh rie • ning/ ehn kvee • teh • ring* |

| That was a very good meal. | **Det var meget lækker mad.** *deh vah mie • erdh lehg • gah madh* |
| I've already paid. | **Jeg har allerede betalt.** *yie hah a • ler • redher beh • ta • lt* |

For Numbers, see page 20.

MEALS & COOKING

> **Morgenmad** (breakfast) is usually eaten quite early, since school and work often begin at 8:00 a.m. A typical breakfast includes buttered bread, **skæreost** (sliced cheese), creamy white cheese like Havarti, jam and coffee. **Frokost** (lunch) is often a simple meal of buttered bread and spreads. **Aftensmad** (dinner) begins at about 6:00 p.m. and is the main meal, as well as the only hot meal, of the day. Dinner may include several courses or may simply be a hearty soup followed by dessert.

BREAKFAST

appelsinjuice	orange juice
ah • berl • seen • djoos	
appelsinmarmelade	orange marmalade
ah • berl • seen • mah • mer • la • dher	
bacon og æg	bacon and eggs
bay • kohn ow ayg	
brød	bread
brurdh	
blødkogt/hårdkogt æg	soft-/hard-boiled egg
blurdh • kohgd/haw • kohgd ayg	
grapefrugtjuice	grapefruit juice
grayb • froagt • djoos	
havregrød	oatmeal
how • rah grurdh	
honning	honey
hoh • ning	
kaffe...	coffee...
kah • fer...	

kaffeinfri *kah • feh • een • free*	decaffeinated
med mælk *mehdh mehlk*	with milk
sort *soart*	black
(kold/varm) mælk *(kohl/vahm) mehlk*	(cold/hot) milk
omelet *oa • mer • leht*	omelet
pandekager *pa • ner • ka • yah*	pancakes
pølser *purl • sah*	sausage
ristet brød *ris • terdh brurdh*	toast
rundstykker *roan • stur • gah*	rolls
røræg *rur • ayg*	scrambled eggs
smør *smur*	butter
spejlæg *spiel • ayg*	fried eggs

skinke og æg
skin • ger ow ayg

ham and eggs

syltetøj
sewl • der • toi

jam

te med mælk/citron
teh mehdh mehlk/see • troan

tea with milk/lemon

varm chokolade
vahm shoa • koa • la • dher

hot chocolate

yoghurt
yoo • goord

yogurt

APPETIZERS

ansjoser
an • shoa • sah

anchovies

artiskokker
ah • tees • koh • gah

artichokes

aspargeshoveder
a • spahs • hoah • dhah

asparagus tips

champignoner
sham • pin • yong

mushrooms

fyldte tomater
fewl • der toa • ma • dah

stuffed tomatoes

gåselever
gow • ser • lehw • ah

goose liver

kaviar
ka • vee • ah

caviar

(marineret/røget) makrel
(mah • ree • neh • rahdh/roi • erdh)
ma • krehl

(marinated/smoked)
mackerel

muslinger
moos • ling • ah

mussels

oliven (fyldte)
oa • lee • vern (fewl • der)

(stuffed) olives

radiser *rah • dee • sah*	radishes
rollmops *rohl • mops*	pickled herring [rollmops]
røget/graved laks salmon *roi • erdh/grah • verdh lahks*	smoked/cured
salat *sa • lat*	salad
saltkød *sahlt • kurdh*	salted beef slices
sild med løg *seel mehdh loi*	herring with onion
sildesalat *see • ler • sa • <u>lat</u>*	herring salad
skinke *skin • ger*	ham
spegepølse *spi • er • purl • ser*	salami
østers *urs • dahs*	oysters
ål (i gelé) *owl (ee sheh • leh)*	(jellied) eel

SOUP

aspargessuppe   asparagus soup
a • sp<u>ah</u>s • soa • per

champisnonsuppe   mushroom soup
sham • pin • yong • soa • per

frugtsuppe   dried fruit soup,
froagt • soa • per   served chilled or hot

gule ærter   split-pea soup with
<u>goo</u> • ler ehr • dah   salt pork

hønsekødsuppe   chicken and
hurn • ser • kurdhs • soa • per   vegetable soup

hummersuppe   lobster chowder
hoa • mah • soa • per

klar suppe med boller og grønsager   vegetable soup
klah soa • per mehdh boh • lah   with meatballs
ow grurn • sa • yah

kråsesuppe   sweet-sour chicken
kr<u>ow</u> • ser • soa • per   giblets soup

labskoves   hearty stew made
lahb • sgows   with beef, potatoes,
                                           carrots and onions

æblesuppe   apple soup
ay • bler • soa • per

ægte skildpaddesuppe   turtle soup
ayg • der skil • pa • dher • soa • per

øllebrød   soup of rye bread
ur • ler • brurdh   cooked with Danish
                                           beer, sugar and
                                           lemon

Soup is, on many occasions, a meal on its own. If you'd like to try a traditional soup, order **aspargessuppe** (asparagus soup), **gule ærter** (split-pea soup), **frugtsuppe** (fruit soup) or chicken soup **med boller** (with meatballs).

FISH & SEAFOOD

aborre	perch
a • bohr	
ansjoser	anchovies
an • shoa • sah	
ål (i gelé/røget)	(jellied/smoked) eel
owl (ee sheh • leh/roi • erdh)	
blåmuslinger	mussels
blaw • moos • ling • ah	
forel	trout
foh • rehl	
gedde	pike
geh • dher	
helleflynder	halibut
heh • ler • flur • nah	

hummer	lobster
hoa • mah	
karpe	carp
ka<u>ah</u> • per	
kaviar	caviar
ka • vee • ah	
krebs	crab
krehbs	
laks	salmon
lahks	
makrel	mackerel
ma • krehl	
piahvar	turbot
peeg • vah	
rejer	shrimp [prawns]
rie • ah	
rogn	roe
rown	
rødspætte	plaice
rurdh • spay • der	
sardiner	sardine
sah • dee • nah	
sild	herring
seel	
røget	smoked
roi • erdh	
i lage	marinated in brine
ee <u>la</u> • yer	
marineret	marinated
mah • ree • neh • rerdh	
skrubbe	flounder
skroa • ber	
store rejer	jumbo shrimp
stoa • ah rie • ah	[prawns]

stør	sturgeon
stur	
søtunge	sole
sur • toang • er	
torsk	cod
tohsk	
tunfisk	tuna
toon • fisk	
ørred	trout
ur • erdh	
østers	oysters
urs • dahs	
ål	eel
owl	

MEAT & POULTRY

and	duck
an	
bacon	bacon
bay • kohn	
blodpølse	black pudding
bloadh • purl • ser	

bøftartar
burf • tah • tah

beef tartare

brisler
brees • lah

sweetbreads

due
doo • er

pigeon

dyrekød
dew • er • kurdh

venison

fasan
fa • san

pheasant

forloren skildpadde
foh • loarn skil • pa • dher

'mock turtle': a very traditional Danish dish consisting of meat from a calf's head with meatballs and fish balls

frikadeller
fri • ka • deh • lah

small meat patties

fårekød
faw • er • kurdh

mutton

grisehoved/grisetæer
gree • ser • hoa • wedh/gree • ser • tehr

pig's head/feet

grydesteg
grew • dher • stie

pot roast

gås
gows

goose

hakkebøf
hah • ker • burf

ground beef patty

hamburgerryg
hahm • boh • rurg

smoked, salted pork with cucumber sauce

hare
hah • rer

hare

kalkun
kal • koon

turkey

kalvebrissel
kal • ver • bree • serl

veal cutlet

kalvekød
kal • ver • kurdh

veal

kanin
ka • neen

rabbit

koldt kødpålæg
kohlt kurdh • paw • laygh

cold cuts

kylling
kew • ling

chicken

kødboller
kurdh • boh • lah

small meatballs, usually served in soup or with pasta

lam
lahm

lamb

lever
leh • wah

liver

leverpaté
leh • wah • pa • teh

liver paté

medisterpølse
meh • dees • dah • purl • ser

spiced pork sausage

oksehale
ohk • ser • ha • ler

oxtail

oksekød *ohk • ser • kurdh*	beef
oksesteg *ohk • ser • stie*	roast beef
pattegris *pa • der • grees*	suckling pig
perlehøne *pehr • ler • hur • ner*	guinea fowl
pølse *purl • sah*	sausage
rensdyr *rehns • dewr*	reindeer
skinke *skin • ger*	ham
sprængt oksebryst *sprehngt ohk • ser • brurst*	boiled, salted brisket of beef
svinekød *sv<u>ee</u> • ner • kurdh*	pork
ung and *oang an*	duckling
vagtel *vahg • derl*	quail
vildsvin *veel • sveen*	wild boar

ⓘ

Smørrebrød (open-faced sandwiches), comprised of buttered rye bread and sliced meat or cheese, have been a part of Danish cuisine for a long time; however, the fancier, more elaborate **smørrebrød** eaten on festive occasions appeared only in the late 1800s. Today **smørrebrød** is topped with a variety of delicacies: mounds of shrimp, eel, smoked salmon, marinated or smoked herring, liver paste, roast beef or pork and steak tartare. The sandwich is then garnished with a number of other ingredients: raw onions, cress, scrambled eggs, egg yolk, radishes, chives and pickled cucumbers to name a few. Many large restaurants serve **smørrebrød**. You can select a traditional combination such as **dyrlægens natmad** (liver paté, corned beef and aspic **smørrebrød**), **rullepølse** (spiced meat roll) or **stjerneskud** (fish and shrimp **smørrebrød**), or you can name the individual items that you prefer.

VEGETABLES & STAPLES

agurk *a • goork*	cucumber
artiskokker *ah • tees • koh • kah*	artichokes
asparges *a • spahs*	asparagus
aubergine *oa • behr • sheen*	eggplant [aubergine]
avocado *a • vo • ka • doa*	avocado
blandede urter *bla • ner • dher oor • dah*	mixed herbs

blomkål	cauliflower
blom • kowl	
...bønner	...beans
...bur • nah	
brune	kidney
br<u>oo</u> • ner	
grønne	green
grur • ner	
hvide	butter
vee • dher	
broccoli	broccoli
broh • koa • lee	
brød	bread
brurdh	
franskbrød	white bread
frahnsk • brurdh	
fuldkornsbrød	whole-grain bread
fool • koarns • brurdh	
pumpernikkel-brød	pumpernickel bread
poom • pah • ni • kerl • brurdh	
rugbrød	rye bread
roo • brurdh	
brøndkarse	watercress
brurn • kah • ser	

champienoner *shahm • peen • yong • ah*	mushrooms
courgette *koor • sheh • ter*	zucchini [courgette]
græskar *grehs • kah*	pumpkin
gulerødder *goo • ler • rur • dhah*	carrots
hvidløg *veedh • loi*	garlic
ingefær *ing • er • fayr*	ginger
julesalat *yoo • ler • sa • lat*	endive [chickory]
kapers *ka • pers*	capers
kartofler *ka • tohf • lah*	potatoes
kastanjer *ka • stan • yah*	chestnuts
kål *kowl*	cabbage
linser *'in • sah*	lentils

løg *loi*	onions
majs *mies*	corn
mel *mehl*	flour
nudler *noodh•lah*	noodles
pasta *pa•sta*	pasta
peber *peh•wah*	pepper (spice)
peberfrugt *peh•wah•froagt*	peppers
peberrod *peh•wah•roadh*	horseradish
porrer *poa•rah*	leeks
radiser *rah•dee•sah*	radishes
ris *rees*	rice
roer *roa•ah*	turnip

rosenkål *roa • sern • kowl*	Brussels sprouts
rødbeder *rurdh • beh • dhah*	beets [beetroot]
salat *sa • lat*	lettuce
selleri *seh • ler • ree*	celery
skalotteløg *ska • loh • der • loi*	shallot
spansk peber *spansk peh • wah*	pimiento pepper
spinat *spee • nat*	spinach
søde kartofler *sur • dher ka • tohf • lah*	sweet potatoes
tomater *toa • ma • dah*	tomatoes
ærter *ehr • dah*	peas

Measurements in Europe are metric – and that applies to the weight of food too. If you tend to think in pounds and ounces, it's worth brushing up on what the equivalent is before you go shopping for fruit and veg in markets and supermarkets. Five hundred grams, or half a kilo, is a common quantity to order, and that converts to just over a pound (17.65 ounces, to be precise).

FRUIT

abrikoser	apricots
ah • bree • koa • sah	
ananas	pineapple
a • na • nas	
appelsin	orange
ah • berl • seen	
banan	banana
ba • nan	
blommer	plums
bloh • mah	
blåbær	blueberries
blaw • behrr	
citron	lemon
see • troan	
dadler	dates
dadh • lah	
fersken	peach
fehrs • gern	
figner	figs
feey • nah	
grapefrugt	grapefruit
grayb • froagt	
hasselnøddur	hazelnuts
ha • serl • nurdh • ah	
hindbær	raspberries
hin • behr	
jordbær	strawberries
yoar • behr	
jordnødder	peanuts
yoar • nurdh • ah	
kastanjer	chestnuts
ka • stan • yah	

kirsebær *keer • ser • behr*	cherries
lime *liem*	lime
mandarin *man • da • reen*	tangerine
mandler *man • lah*	almonds
melon *meh • loan*	melon
nektarin *nehk • tah • reen*	nectarine
pære *pay • rah*	pear
rabarber *rah • bah • bah*	rhubarb
rosiner *roa • see • nah*	raisins
solbær *soal • behr*	black currants
stikkelsbær *sti • gerls • behr*	gooseberries
tyttebær *tew • der • behr*	cranberries

valnødder	walnuts
val • nur • dha	
vandmelon	watermelon
van • meh • loan	
vindruer	grapes
*v**ee**n • droo • ah*	
æble	apple
__ay__ • bler	

CHEESE

danablu	Danish blue cheese
*d__a__ • na • bl**oo***	
danbo	mild, firm cheese,
dan • boa	sometimes
	with caraway seeds
elbo	hard cheese with
ehl • boa	a delicate taste
esrom	strong, slightly
ehs • roam	aromatic cheese
maribo	soft, mild cheese
mah • ree • boa	
molbo	rich and highly
mohl • boa	flavored

mycella
mew • seh • la

similar to Danish blue cheese, but milder

ost
oast

cheese

samsø
sahm • sur

mild, firm cheese with a sweet, nutty flavor

DESSERT

appelsinfromage
ah • berl • seen • froa • ma • sher

orange mousse

bondepige med slør
boa • ner • pee • er mehdh slur

'veiled countrymaid': bread crumbs, apple sauce, cream, sugar

brune kager
broo • ner ka • yah

spicy, crispy cookies [biscuits] with almond

citronfromage
see • troan • froa • ma • sher

lemon mousse

flødekage
flur • dher • ka • yer

cream cake

fromage
froa • ma • sher

mousse

is
ees

ice cream

kage
ka • yer

cake

karamelrand
kah • rah • mehl • rehn

caramel custard

pandekager
pa • ner • ka • yah

thin pancakes

rødgrød med fløde
rurdh • grurdh mehdh flur • dher

fruit jelly served with cream

små pandekager	fritters
smow pa•ner•ka•yah	
småkager	cookies [biscuits]
smaw•ka•yer	
æblekage med rasp og flødeskum	layers of stewed
ay•ble•ka•yer mehdh rahsp ow	apple and cookie
fl<u>ur</u>•dher•skoam	crumbs topped with
	whipped cream

SAUCES & CONDIMENTS

salt	salt
salt	
peber	pepper
pe•wer	
sennep	mustard
seh•nerp	
ketchup	ketchup
ket•youp	

YOU MAY HEAR...

Kan jeg hjælpe dig?	Can I help you?
kan yie yehl•per die	
Hvad skulle det være?	What would you
vadh skoo deh v<u>ay</u>•ah	like?
Skulle der være andet?	Anything else?
skoo dah v<u>ay</u>•ah a•nerdh	
Det bliver...kroner.	That's...kroner
deh bleer...kroa•nah	

In Denmark, there are a few supermarket chains in
addition to many local markets located in every city and
town. Not all supermarkets accept international credit cards;
some accept only **Dankort** (the special Danish equivalent of
credit and debit cards). So remember to bring cash when you
go shopping for groceries.

AT THE MARKET

Where are the trolleys/baskets?	**Hvor er vognene/kurvene?** *voar ehr v<u>ow</u> • ner • ner/koor • ver • ner*
Where is?	**Hvor er...?** *voar ehr...*
I'd like some of that/those.	**Jeg vil gerne have noget af det/nogle af dem.** *yie vil gehr • ner ha n<u>oa</u> • erdh a deh/ noa • ler a dehm*
Can I taste it?	**Må jeg smage det?** *mow yie sm<u>a</u> • yer deh*
I'd like.	**Jeg vil gerne have...** *yie vil gehr • ner ha...*

a kilo/half-kilo of… **et kilo/halvt kilo…**
eht kee • loa/halt kee • lo…

a liter/half-liter of… **en liter/halv liter…**
ehn lee • dah/hal lee • dah…

a piece of. **et stykke…**
eht stur • ger…

a slice of. **en skive…**
ehn skee • ver…

More/Less than that. **Mere/Mindre end det.**
meh • ah/min • drah ehn deh

How much? **Hvor meget koster det?**
voar mie • erdh kos • dah deh

Where do I pay? **Hvor kan jeg betale?**
voar kan yie beh • ta • ler

Can I have a bag? **Kan jeg få en bærepose?**
kan yie fow ehn bay • rah • poa • ser

I'm being helped. **Jeg bliver ekspederet.**
yie blee • vah ehks • peh • deh • rahdh

For Money, see page 30.

For Money, see page 30.

YOU MAY SEE…

MINDST HOLDBAR TIL…	best if used by…
KALORIER	calories
FEDTFRI	fat free
OPBEVARES I KØLESKAB	keep refrigerated
SIDSTE SALGSDATO	sell by
EGNET FOR VEGETARER	suitable for vegetarians

IN THE KITCHEN

bottle opener	**oplukker**
	ohb • loag • gah
bowls	**skåle**
	sk<u>ow</u> • ler
can opener	**dåseåbner**
	d<u>ow</u> • ser • ow • bnah
corkscrew	**proptrækker**
	prohb • treh • kah
cups	**kopper**
	koh • bah
forks	**gafler**
	gahf • lah
frying pan	**stegepande**
	stie • yer • pa • ner
glasses	**glas**
	glas
knives	**knive**
	kn<u>ee</u> • ver
measuring cup/	**målekrus/måleske**
spoon	*m<u>ow</u> • ler • kr<u>oo</u>s/m<u>ow</u> • ler • skeh*
napkins	**servietter**
	sehr • vee • eh • dah
plates	**tallerkner**
	ta • l<u>eh</u>rk • nah
pot	**gryde**
	gr<u>ew</u> • dher
saucepan	**kasserolle**
	ka • ser • rohl • ler
spatula	**spatel**
	sp<u>a</u> • derl
spoons	**skeer**
	skeh • ah

For Domestic Items, see page 80.

DRINKS

NEED TO KNOW

May I see the wine list/drink menu?	**Må jeg se vinlisten/listen med drinks?** *mow yie seh veen • lis • tern/lis • tern mehdh drinks*
What do you recommend?	**Hvad kan du anbefale?** *vadh kan doo an • beh • fa • ler*
I'd like a bottle/ glass of red/white wine.	**Jeg vil gerne bede om en flaske/et glas rødvin/hvidvin.** *yie vil gehr • ner beh ohm ehn flas • ger/eht glas rurdh • veen/ veedh • veen*
The house wine, please.	**Hustes vin, tak.** *hoo • sets veen tahk*
Another bottle/ glass, please.	**En flaske/Et glas mere, tak.** *ehn flas • ger/ eht glas meh • ah tahk*
I'd like a local beer.	**Jeg vil gerne bede om en lokal øl.** *yie vil gehr • ner beh ohm ehn loa • kal url*
Let me buy you a drink.	**Lad mig byde dig på en drink.** *ladh mie bew • dher die paw ehn drink*
Cheers!	**Skål!** *skowl*
A coffee/tea, please.	**En kop kaffe/te, tak.** *ehnkohpkah • fer/teh tahk*
With milk.	**Med mælk.** *mehdh mehlk*

With sugar.	**Med sukker.**
	mehdh soa • gah
With artificial	**Med sødemiddel.**
sweetener.	*mehdh sur • dher • mee • dherl*
...please.	**...tak.**
	...tahk
Juice	**Juice**
	djoos
Soda	**Sodavand**
	soa • da • van
Sparkling/	**Danskvand/Kildevand**
Still water	*dansk • van/kee • ler • van*

NON-ALCOHOLIC DRINKS

appelsinjuice	orange juice
ah • berl • seen • djoos	
grapefrugtjuice	grapefruit juice
grayb • froagt • djoos	
kaffe	coffee
kah • fer	
limonade	lemonade
• moh • na • dher	
mineralvand	mineral water
mee • neh • rahl • van	
mælk	milk
mehlk	
te	tea
teh	
tomatjuice	tomato juice
oa • mat • djoos	

varm chokolade   hot chocolate
*vah*m *shoa • koa • la • dher*
æblejuice   apple juice
ay • bler • djoos

If you're not in the mood for Danish beer, there are
a number of other drinks to enjoy. Strong filtered coffee
is enjoyed throughout the day, even with meals. If you
prefer tea, herbal tea is growing in popularity. **Varm
chokolade** (hot chocolate) is often served to children, but
is also enjoyed by adults. For a unique drink, you could
try **hyldeblomstsaft** (elderflower juice), a delicacy that
is making a comeback. Or, if you simply prefer water, try
danskvand or **mineralvand** (sparking or mineral water)
with a bit of citrus fruit.

YOU MAY HEAR...

Må jeg byde på en drink?
mow yie bew • dher paw ehn drienk
Can I get you a drink?

Med mælk eller sukker?
medh mehlk ehl • er sug • gar
With milk or sugar?

Vand meller eller uden brus?
van medh ehl • er udhen bruus
Sparkling or still water?

APERITIFS, COCKTAILS & LIQUEURS

akvavit
ah • kva • veet
aquavit

aperitif
ah • peh • ree • teef
aperitif

cognac
kon • yahk
brandy

gin
djin
gin

kalvados
kal • va • dohs
apple brandy

Akvavit is a very popular drink in Denmark. Like vodka, it's distilled from potatoes, though barley is also used. The color varies according to the herbs and spices with which the drink is flavored.
Often served with a beer chaser, **akvavit** is drunk ice-cold, and makes an ideal accompaniment to Danish appetizers.

kirsebærcognac	cherry brandy
keer • se • bayr • kon • yahk	
likør	liquer
lee • kur	
portvin	port wine
poart • veen	
rom	rum
rohm	
snaps	schnapps
snahps	
vermouth	vermouth
vehr • moot	
vodka	vodka
vohd • ka	
...whisky	...whisky
...wis • keei	
tør	neat (straight)
tur	
med isterninger	on the rocks
mehdh ees • tehr • ning • ah	
med lidt vand	with a little water
mehdh lit van	
med soda	with soda water
mehdh soa • da	

BEER

En flaske...   A bottle of...
ehn flas•ger...
En pilsner, tak.   A pilsner, please.
ehn pils•nah tahk
Et glas...   A glass of...
eht glas...

  fadøl   draft [draught] beer
  fadh•url
  udenlandsk øl   imported beer
  <u>oo</u>•dhern•lansk url
  lys/mørk øl   light/dark beer
  lews/murrk url
  alkoholfri øl   non-alcoholic beer
  alkho•hohl•free urhl

(i)

The Carlsberg and Tuborg breweries are internationally known; however, Denmark has many microbreweries that offer a variety of refreshing beer options. If you feel like trying something new, taste one of the local brews.

A special event every year is **J-day**, whose name comes from the Danish word **Juleøl** (Christmas beer). **J-day** is normally celebrated the first Friday in November, when, at exactly 8:59 p.m., all the Danish breweries release their special, limited edition Christmas beer. Each company creates a new recipe each year. That evening you'll find pubs filled with people enjoying their first beer of the Christmas season. **Skål!** (Cheers!)

WINE

..vin	...wine
...veen	
hvid	white
veedh	
mousserende	sparkling
moo • seh • rern • der	
rosé	rosé
roa • seh	
rød	red
rurdh	
sød	sweet
surdh	
tør	dry
tur	
champagne	champagne
cham • pan • ye	
dessertvin	dessert wine
des • serht • veen	
husets vin	house/table
hoo • serdhs veen	

ON THE MENU

aborre	perch
ah • bohr	
abrikoser	apricots
ah • bree • koa • sah	
afkølet	chilled
ow • kur • lerdh	

agerhøne
a • yer • hur • ner

roast partridge
served with red
currant jam or apple
sauce and
horseradish

agurk
a • goork

cucumber

agurksalat
a • goork • sa • lat

cucumber in vinegar
dressing

ananas
a • na • nas

pineapple

and
an

duck

and, stegt
an stehgt

roast duck stuffed
with chestnuts or
apples and prunes,
served with olive or
mushroom sauce

anisfrø
a • nees • frur

aniseed

ansjoser
an • shoa • sah

anchovies

aperitif
ah • peh • ree • teef

aperitif

appelsin
ah • berl • seen
orange

appelsinfromage
ah • berl • seen • froa • ma • sher
orange mousse

appelsinmarmelade
ah • berl • seen • mah • mer • la • dher
marmalade

appelsinsovs
ah • berl • seen • sows
orange sauce

artiskokker
ah • tees • koh • gah
artichokes

asier
a • shah
pickled gherkins

asparges
a • spahs
asparagus

aspargeshoveder
a • spahs • hoh • dhah
asparagus tips

aspargessuppe
a • spahs • soa • per
asparagus soup

aubergine
oaber • sheen
eggplant [aubergine]

avocado
a • vo • ka • doa
avocado

bacon
bay • kohn
bacon

banan
ba • nan

banana

basilikum
ba • see • lee • koam

basil

bearnaisesovs
behr • nays • sows

a cream sauce
flavored with
tarragon and vinegar

beef
ohk • ser • kurdh

oksekød

blandede grøntsager
bla • ner • dher grun • sa • yer

mixed vegetables

blandede urter
bla • ner • dher • oor • dah

mixed herbs

blandet hors d'oeuvre
bla • nerdh ohr durv • rah

assorted appetizers

blodpølse
bloadh • purl • sah

black pudding

blomkål
blohm • kowl

cauliflower

blommer
bloh • mah

plums

blå foreller
blaw foa • reh lah

poached trout,serve
with boiled potatoes,
melted butter,
horseradish and
lemon

blåbær
blaw • behr

blueberries

blåmuslinger
blaw • moos • ling • ah

mussels

boller i karry
boh • lah ee kah • ree

meatballs in a curry
sauce

bondepige med slør
boh • ner • pee • yer mehdh slur

'veiled country maid':
a mixtureof bread
crumbs, apple
sauce, cream and
sugar

brisler
brees • lah

sweetbreads

broccoli
broh • koa • lee

broccoli

brun sovs
broon sows

traditional thick
gravy

brune kager
*br**oo** • ner ka • yah*

spicy, crisp cookies
[biscuits] with
almonds

brunede kartofler
*br**oo** • ner • dher ka • tohf • lah*

caramelized
potatoes

brød
brurdh

bread

brøndkarse
*brurn • **kah** • ser*

watercress

burger
bur • gah

burger

bøftartar
*burf • tah • **tah***

beef tartare

bønner
bur • nah

beans

champignoner
shahm • peen • yohng • ah

mushrooms

champignonsuppe
sham • peen • yohng • so • per

mushroom soup

chili
tjee • lee

chili

(varm) chokolade
(vahm) shoa • koa • la • dher

(hot) chocolate

chokoladeis
shoa • koa • la • dher • ees

chocolate ice cream

chutney smør
tjoht • nee smur

chutney butter

citron
see • troan

lemon

citronfromage
see • troan • froa • ma • sher

lemon mousse

citronmarinade
see • troan • mah • ree • na • dher

marinade of lemon, oil, salt and pepper, paprika, herbs

citronsaft
see • troan • sahft

lemon juice

cognac
kohn • yahk

cognac

courgette
koor • sheh • der

zucchini [courgette]

dadler
dadh • lah

dates

danablu
da • na • bloo

Danish blue cheese

danbo
dan • boa

a mild, firm cheese, sometimes with caraway seeds

desserter
deh • sehr • tah

desserts

dild
deel

dill

drikkevarer
drig • ger • vah • rah

beverages

due
doo • er

pigeon

dyrekød
dew • rer • kurdh

venison

dyreryg
dew • rer • rurg

saddle (cut of meat)

eddike
eh • dhee • ker

vinegar

elbo
ehl • boa

a hard cheese with a delicate taste

engelsk bøf
ehng • erlsk burf

fillet of beef with onions and boiled potatoes

esrom
ehs • roam

a strong, slightly aromatic cheese of spongy texture

estragon *eh • strah • gong*	tarragon
fadøl *fadh • url*	draft [draught] beer
fasan *fa • san*	pheasant
fennikel *feh • nee • kerl*	fennel
fersken *fehrs • gern*	peach
figner *feey • nah*	figs
fisk *fisk*	fish
fjerkræ *fyehr • kray*	poultry
flaskeøl *flas • ger • url*	bottled beer
flæskesteg med svær *flay • sger • stie mehdh svehr*	roast pork with crackling
flødekage *flur • dher • ka • yer*	cream cake
flødepeberrod *flur • dher • peh • wah • roadh*	horseradish cream dressing
forel *foa • rehl*	trout
forloren skildpadde *foh • loh • rern skil • pa • dher*	'mock turtle': a very traditional Danish dish consisting of meat, meatballs and fish balls
franskbrød *frahnsk • brurdh*	white bread
frikadeller *fri • ka • dehl • lah*	meatballs

fromage	mousse
froa • ma • sher	
frugt	fruit
froagt	
frugtsuppe	fruit soup, composed
froagt • soa • per	of a variety of dried
	fruits, served
	chilled or hot
fuldkornsbrød	whole-grain bread
fool • koarns • brurdh	
fyldte tomater	stuffed tomatoes
fewl • der toh • ma • dah	
fårekød	mutton
faw • er • kurdh	
gedde	pike
geh • dher	
gin	gin
djin	
grapefrugt	grapefruit
grayb • froagt	
grillstegt kylling	barbecued chicken
greel • stehgt kew • ling	
grisehoved	pig's head
gree • ser • ho • wedh	
grisetæer	pig's feet
gree • ser • tehr	
grydedesteg	pot roast
grew • dher • stie	
græskar	pumpkin
grehs • kah	
grønne bønner	green beans
grurn • ner bur • nah	
grøntsager	vegetables
grurn • sa • yah	

gule ærter *g<u>oo</u> • ler ehr • dah*	split-pea soup with salt pork
gulerødder *goo • ler • rur • dhah*	carrots
gås *gows*	goose
gåselever *g<u>ow</u> • ser • leh • wah*	goose liver
hakkebøf *hah • ger • burf*	beef patties
hamburgerryg *hahm • boh • rurg*	smoked, salted saddle of pork, roasted and served in thin slices with Cumberland (cucumber-based) sauce
hare *h<u>ar</u> • rer*	hare
hasselnødder *ha • serl • nur • dhah*	hazelnuts
havregrød *how • er • grurdh*	porridge

helleflynder	halibut
heh • ler • flew • nah	
hindbær	raspberries
hin • behr	
honning	honey
hoh • ning	
hummer	lobster
hoa • mah	
hummersuppe	lobster chowder
hoa • mah • soa • per	
hvidløg	garlic
veedh • loi	
hvidvinssovs	white wine sauce
veedh • veens • sows	
hønsekødsuppe	chicken and
hurn • ser • kurdhs • soa • per	vegetable soup
hårdkogt	hard-boiled
haw • kohgtt	
ingefær	ginger
ing • er • fehr	
is	ice cream
ees	

italiensk salat
ee • tal • yehnsk sa • lat

diced carrots and asparagus, green peas and mayonnaise

jordbær
yoar • behr

strawberries

jordbæris
yoar • behr • ees

strawberry ice cream

jordnødder
yoar • nur • dhah

peanuts

juice
djoos

juice

julesalat
yoo • ler • sa • lat

endive

kaffe
kah • fer

coffee

kaffeinfri
kah • feh • een • free

decaffeinated

kage
ka • yer

cake

kalkun
kal • koon

turkey

kalkunragout
kal • koon rah • goo

turkey in a sweet-and-sour gravy, served with mashed potatoes or a chestnut purée

kalvebrissel
kal • ver • bris • serl

calf's sweetbread

kalvekød
kal • ver • kurdh

veal

kanel
ka • nehl

cinnamon

kanin
ka • neen

rabbit

kanin i flødepeberrod
ka • neen ee flur • dher • peh • wah • roadh
rabbit stew with horseradish cream dressing, roast mushroom and onions

kapers
ka • pahs
capers

karaffel
ka • rah • ferl
carafe

karamelrand
kah • rah • mehl • ran
caramel custard

karpe
kah • per
carp

kartoffel croquettes
ka • toh • ferl kroa • keh • dah
potato croquettes

kartoffelmos (med æbler)
ka • toh • ferl • moas (mehdh ay • blah)
mashed potatoes (with apple purée)

kartoffelsalat
ka • toh • ferl • sa • lat
potato salad

kartofler
ka • tohf • lah
potatoes

kastaniesovs
ka • stan • yer • sows
chestnut sauce

kastanjer
ka • stan • yah
chestnuts

kaviar
ka • vee • ah
caviar

kirsebær
keer • ser • behr
cherries

kirsebærcognac
keer • se • bayr • kohn • yahk
cherry brandy

klar suppe med boller og grønsager
klah soa • per mehdh boh • lah ow grurn • sa • yah
vegetable soup with meatballs

kokosnød *k<u>oa</u> • kohs • nurdh*	coconut
koldt bord *kohlt boar*	smorgasbord
koldt kødpålæg *kolt kurdh • paw • laygh*	cold cuts
kommen *koh • mern*	cumin
kotelet *koa • der • leht*	chop, cutlet
krebs *krehbs*	crab
kryddernellike *kr<u>ew</u> • dher • neh • lee • ker*	clove
kråsesuppe *kr<u>ow</u> • ser • soa • per*	a sweet-sour chicken giblets soup, often with dried apples
kvæde *kv<u>ay</u> • dher*	quince
kylling *rew • ling*	chicken

kylling med rejer og asparges
kew • ling mehdh rie • ah ow a • spahs

chicken in an asparagus sauce and garnished with shrimp

kyllingesalat
kew • ling • er • sa • lat

chicken, macaroni, tomato, peppers, olives, peas, lettuce and mushrooms, covered with a tomato dressing

kød
kurdh

meat

kødboller
kurdh • boh • lah

meatballs

labskovs
lahb • skows

beef, diced potatoes, slices of carrots and onions, served with rye bread

lagkage
lahw • ka • yer

layer cake

laks
lahks

salmon

lam
lahm

lamb

laurbærblad	bay leaf
lah • wer • behr • bla • dher	
lever	liver
leh • wah	
likør	liqueur
lee • kur	
lime	lime
liem	
limonade	lemonade
li • moa • na • dhcr	
linser	lentils
lin • sah	
lys hvidtøl	a pale, sweetish, low-alcohol beer
lews veed • url	
løg	onions
loi	
løgsovs	onion sauce
loi • sows	
majroer	turnips
mie • roa • ah	
majs	corn
mies	
makrel	mackerel
ma • krehl	
makrelsalat	mackerel in tomato sauce topped with mayonnaise
ma • krehl • sa • lat	
maltøl	a very heavy beer, regarded as a tonic
malt • url	
mandarin	tangerine
man • da • reen	
mandelgræskar	vegetable marrow
ma • nerl • grehs • kar	
mandler	almonds
man • lah	

maribo *mah • ree • boa*	a soft, mild cheese
marineret *mah • ree • n<u>eh</u> • rerdh*	marinated
medisterpølse *meh • dees • dah • purl • sah*	spiced pork sausage, served with stewed vegetables or sautéed cabbage and potatoes
medium *m<u>eh</u> • dee • oam*	medium
mel *mehl*	flour
melon *meh • <u>loa</u>n*	melon
merian *m<u>eh</u> • ree • an*	marjoram
milkshake *meelk • sjayk*	milkshake
mineralvand *mee • mer • <u>rah</u>l • van*	mineral water
molbo *mol • boa*	like Edam; a rich and highly flavored cheese

mousserende
moo • seh • rern • der

sparkling (wine)

muskatnød
moo • skat • nurdh

nutmeg

muslinger
moos • ling • ah

mussels

mycella
mew • sehl • la

similar to Danishblue
cheese, but milder

mynte
mewn • der

mint

mælk
mehlk

milk

mørkt hvidtøl
murkt veed • url

a dark beer; sweet
and creamy

nektarin
nehk • tah • reen

nectarine

nudler
noodh • lah

noodles

nye kartofler
new • er ka • tohf • lah

new potatoes

nyrer
new • rah

kidneys

oksefilet
ohk • ser • fee • leh

fillet

oksehale
ohk • ser • ha • ler

oxtail

oksemørbrad
ohk • ser • mur • brahdh

tenderloin

oksesteg
ohk • ser • stie

roast beef

oksetyndsteg
ohk • ser • turn • stie

sirloin

oliven (fyldte)
oa • lee • vern (fewl • der)

olives (stuffed)

omelet
oa • mer • leht

omelet

oregano
oh • reh • ga • noa

oregano

ost
oast

cheese

ovnstegt
own • stehght

roast

pandekager
pa • ner • ka • yah

pancakes

paprika
pahp • ree • ka

paprika

pasta
pa • sta

pasta

pattegris
pah • der • grees

suckling pig

peber
peh • wah

pepper (spice)

peberfrugt
peh • wah • froagt

pepper (vegetable)

peberrod
pehr • wah • roadh

horseradish

perlehøne
pehr • ler • hur • ner

guinea fowl

persille
pehr • see • ler

parsley

persillesovs
pehr • see • ler • sows

parsley sauce

pighvar
peeg • vah

turbot

pocheret æg
poa • sheh • rerdh ayg

poached eggs

pommes frites
pohm freet

French fries [chips]

porrer
poa • ah

leeks

portvin	port wine
poart • veen	
pumpernikkel-brød	pumpernickel bread
pohm • bah • ni • ker • brurdh	
purløg	chives
poor • loi	
pære	pear
bay • ah	
pølse	sausage
burl • ser	
rabarber	rhubarb
rah • bah • bah	
radiser	radishes
rah • dee • sah	
ragout	stew
ra • goo	
rejer	shrimp [prawns]
rie • ah	
remoulade	mustard and herb
eh • moa • la • dher	cream dressing
rensdyr	reindeer
rehns • dewr	
ribbenssteg	ribsteak
ee • behns • stie	

rice	rice
*ree*s	
ristet brød	toast
ris • terdh brurdh	
roer	turnips
r<u>oa</u> • ah	
rogn	roe
rown	
rollmops	pickled herring
rol • mohps	[rollmops]
rom	rum
rohm	
rosé	rosé
roa • s<u>eh</u>	
rosemarin	rosemary
roas • mah • r<u>ee</u>n	
rosenkål	Brussels sprouts
r<u>oa</u> • sern • kowl	
rosiner	raisins
roa • s<u>ee</u> • nah	
rugbrød	rye bread
roo • brurdh	
rundstykker	rolls
roan • stur • gah	

rype
rew • per

grouse

røget sild
roi • erdh seel

smoked herring

røræg
rur • ayg

scrambled eggs

rørt smør
rurt smur

flavored cream
butter

safran
sa • fran

saffron

salat
sa • lat

salad; lettuce

salt
salt

salt

saltagurk
salt • a • goork

pickles

saltkød
salt • kurdh

salt beef slices

salvie
sal • vee • er

sage

samsø
sahm • sur

a mild, firm cheese
with a sweet, nutty
flavor

sardiner
sah • dee • nah

sardines

selleri
seh • leh • ree

celery

sellerisalat
seh • lebi • ree • sa • lat

celery salad with a
cheese dressing or
mayonnaise

sellerisovs
seh • leh • ree • sows

celery-flavored sauce
with sherry

sennep
seh • nerp

mustard

sennepssovs
seh • nerps • sows
mustard sauce

sild
seel
herring

sild i karry
seel ee kah • ree
herring in curry
sauce

sild med løg
seel mehdh loi
herring with onion

sild, røget
seel roi • erdh
herring, smoked, on
dark rye bread,
garnished with a raw
egg yolk, radishes
and chives

sildesalat
see • ler • sa • lat
marinated or pickled
herring, beet, apple
and pickles in a spicy
dressing

skaldyr
skal • dewr
seafood

skalotteløg
ska • loh • ter • loi
shallot

skank
skahnk
shank

skibsøl
skeebs • url
dark 'ship's beer'
noted for its smoked-
-malt-character

skidne æg
skeedh • ner ayg
poached or hard-
boiled eggs
in a cream sauce,
with fish and mustard

skinke
skin • ger
ham

skinke og æg
skin • ger ow ayg
ham and eggs

skrubbe *skroa • ber*	flounder
smør *smur*	butter
smørrebrød *smur • er • brurdh*	famous Danish open-faced sandwich
små pandekager *smow pa • ner • ka • yah*	fritters
småkager *smow • ka • yah*	cookies [biscuits]
solbær *soal • behr*	black currants
spansk peber *spansk peh • wah*	pimiento pepper
spegepølse *spie • er • purl • ser*	salami
spejlæg *spiel • ayg*	fried eggs
spinat *spee • nat*	spinach
spiseolie *spee • ser • oal • yer*	oil
sprængt oksebryst *sprayngt ohk • ser • brurst*	boiled, salted beef brisket

spækket steg *speh • gerdh stie*	larded roast
stærk salatsovs *stehrk sa • lat • sows*	egg yolks, vinegar or lemon juice, oil, salt and pepper or paprika, Worcester sauce, onion or garlic and dill, all mixed with whipped cream
stegte kartofler *stehg • der ka • tohf • lah*	sautéed potatoes
stikkelsbær *sti • kerls • behr*	gooseberries
store rejer *stoa • ah rie • ah*	shrimp [prawns]
stør *stur*	sturgeon
sukker *soa • gah*	sugar
suppe *soa • pah*	soup
sylteagurker *sewl • der • a • goor • kah*	gherkins

syltetøj *sewl • der • toi*	jam
søde kartofler *sur • dher ka • tohf • lah*	sweet potatoes
sødemiddel *sur • dher • mee • dherl*	artificial sweetener
søtunge *sur • toang • ah*	sole
torsk *tohsk*	cod
torsk, kogt *tohsk kohgt*	cod, poached
torskerogn, ristet *tohs • ger • rown ris • terdh*	cod roe, fried
tunfisk *toon • fisk*	tuna
tunge *toang • er*	tongue
tyttebær *tew • der • behr*	cranberries
tørret frugt *tur • erdh froagt*	dried fruit
ung and *oang an*	duckling
vagtel *vahg • derl*	quail
valnødder *val • nur • dhah*	walnuts
vand *van*	water
vandmelon *van • meh • loan*	watermelon
vanilje *va • nil • yer*	vanilla
vegetar *veh • ger • tah*	vegetarian

vermouth	vermouth
vehr • moot	
vildsvin	wild boar
veel • sveen	
vildt	game
veelt	
vildtsovs	sauce of fresh cream
veelt • sows	and red currant jam
vin	wine
veen	
vinaigrette sovs	vinegar and oil
vee • na • greht sows	dressing
vindruer	grapes
veen • droo • ah	
vinkogt laks med pikant sovs	salmon poached in
veen • kogt lahks mehdh pee • kant sows	white wine, dressed
	with a spicy sauce
vodka	vodka
vohd • ka	
whisky	whisky
whis • kee	
ymersovs	lemon juice, spices
ew • mah • sows	and herbs,
	mixed with milk or
	cream
yoghurt	yogurt
yoo • goord	
æble	apple
ay • bler	
æbleflæsk	smoked bacon with
ay • bler • flaysk	onions and sautéed
	apple rings
æblekage med rasp og flødeskum	stewed apples with
ay • bler • ka • yer mehdh rahsp	vanilla served with
ow flur • dher • skoam	layers of cookie
	crumbs and topped
	with whipped cream

æblesuppe
ay • bler • soa • per

apple soup

æg
ayg

egg

æggekage
ay • ger • ka • yer

scrambled eggs with onions, chives, potatoes and bacon

æggesovs
ay • ger • sows

egg sauce

æggeretter
ay • ger • reh • dah

egg dishes

ægte skildpaddesuppe
ehg • der skil • pa • dher • soa • per

turtle soup

øl
url

beer

øllebrød
ur • lah • brurdh

rye bread cooked with Danish beer, sugar and lemon, served with milk and cream

ørred
ur • rerdh

trout

østers
urs • dahs

oysters

ål
owl

eel

ål, stegt med stuvede kartofler
owl stehg mehdh st<u>oo</u> • ver • dher ka • tof • lah

eel, fried, with diced potatoes in a white sauce

ålesuppe
<u>ow</u> • ler • soa • per

sweet-and-sour eel soup, with apples and prunes, served with dark rye bread

GOING OUT

GOING OUT

NEED TO KNOW

What is there to do in the evenings?	**Hvad laver man her om aftenen?** *vadh la • vah man hehr ohm af • tern*
Do you have a program of events?	**Har du et program over arrangementerne?** *hah doo eht proa • grahm ow • ah ah • rahng • sheh • mang • ah • ner*
What's playing at the movies [cinema] tonight?	**Hvad går der i biografen i aften?** *vadh gaw dehr ee bee • oa • gra • fern ee af • tern*
Where's…?	**Hvor er…?** *voar ehr…*
the downtown area	**den indre by** *dehn in • drah bew*
the bar	**baren** *bah • ern*
the dance club	**diskoteket** *dees • koa • teh • kerdh*
Is there a cover charge?	**Koster det noget at komme ind?** *kohs • dah deh noa • erdh ad koh • mer in*

ENTERTAINMENT

Can you recommend…?	**Kan du anbefale…?** *kan doo an • beh • fa • ler…*
a concert	**en koncert** *ehn kohn • sehrt*
a movie	**en film** *ehn film*

(i)

Culturally, there is a lot to enjoy in Denmark. Ballet has been a tradition since the 17th century. The Royal Theater produces plays in a range of genres by both Danish and foreign playwrights. Danish film is also internationally known and has been dominated in recent years by Lars Von Trier.

If you are interested in the visual arts, visit the **Louisiana museum.** Located on the North Zealand coast, it is accessible by car or train. The museum houses an important collection of modern and contemporary art and is located on spectacular seaside property.

an opera	**en opera**
	ehn oa • peh • rah
a play	**et teaterstykke**
	eht teh • a • dah • stur • ger
When does it start/end?	**Hvad tid starter/slutter det?**
	vadh teedh stah • dah/sloo • dah deh
What's the dress code?	**Er der nogen regler for påklædning?**
	ehr dehr noa • ern ray • lah foh pow • klaydh • ning
I like...	**Jeg kan godt lide...**
	yie kan gohd lee...
classical music	**klassisk musik**
	kla • seesk moo • seek
folk music	**folkemusik**
	fohl • ker • moo • seek
jazz	**jazz**
	djas
pop music	**popmusik**
	pohp • moo • seek
rap	**rapmusik**
	rahp • moo • seek

For Tickets, see page 45.

There are countless festivals scheduled throughout the year in Denmark. Tourist information offices, travel agencies, hotels and guide books offer extensive information about local as well as national celebrations. A handful of the annual events include the Copenhagen Marathon, Green Mermaid Festival, Beer Festival, Copenhagen Jazz Festival and Roskilde Festival of rock music. Also, if you're near the coast in June, Midsummer Night, the longest night of the year, is a fun event, traditionally celebrated with bonfires and other festivities.

YOU MAY HEAR...

Sluk venligst din mobiltelefon.
*sloak <u>vehn</u>•leest deen
moa•<u>beel</u>•teh•ler•foan*

Turn off your cell [mobile] phones.

NIGHTLIFE

What is there to do in the evenings?	**Hvad laver man her om aftenen?** *vadh <u>la</u>•vah man hehr ohm <u>af</u>•tern*
Can you recommend...?	**Kan du anbefale...?** *kan doo <u>an</u>•beh•<u>fa</u>•ler...*
a bar	**en bar** *ehn bah*
a casino	**et kasino** *eht ka•<u>see</u>•noa*

ⓘ

A favorite Danish pastime is visiting pubs, though you can also find wine bars and cocktail bars. A traditional pub is called a **bodega** (beer bar). There you'll see Danes enjoying the local brews and playing dice. Dice can be requested at the bar.

Another option is to check out the many **hyggelige** cafes. Cafes range from those where you can order a drink and a simple sandwich to those with sophisticated decor and jet-set clientele.

If you're in the mood for music, there are plenty of dance clubs as well as regular live music shows to be found.

a dance club	**et diskotek** *eht dee • skoa • tehk*
a gay club	**et bøssediskotek** *eht bur • ser • dee • skoa • tehk*
a jazz club	**en jazzklub** *ehn jazz • kluhb*
a club with Danish music	**et spillested med dansk musik** *ehd spee • ler • stedh medh dansk muh • sikh*
a nightclub	**en natklub** *ehn nat • kloob*
Is there live music?	**Er der live musik?** *ehr dehr liev moo • seek*
How do I get there?	**Hvordan kommer jeg derhen?** *voar • dan koh • mah yie dehr • hehn*
Is there a cover charge?	**Koster det noget at komme ind?** *kohs • dah det noa • erdh ad koh • mer in*
Let's go dancing.	**Lad og gå ud og danse.** *ladh ohs gow oodh ow dan • ser*

Is this area safe at night? | **Er dette område sikkert om natten?**
ehr deh • ter ohm • row • dhe sig • gard ohm na • dern

For The Dating Game, see page 235.

ROMANCE

NEED TO KNOW

Would you like to go out for a drink/meal?
Har du lyst til at gå ud og få en drink/noget at spise?
hah doo lurst til ad gow ood ow fow ehn drink/<u>noa</u> • erdh ad sp<u>ee</u> • ser

What are your plans for tonight/tomorrow?
Hvad er dine planer for i aften/i morgen?
vadh ehr <u>dee</u> • ner pl<u>a</u> • nah foh ee <u>ahf</u> • tern/ee <u>mohn</u>

Can I have your number?
Må jeg få dit nummer?
mow yie fow deet <u>noa</u> • mah

Can I join you?
Må jeg komme med dig?
mow yie koh • mer mehdh die

Let me buy you a drink.
Lad mig købe dig en drink.
ladh mie <u>kur</u> • ber die ehn drink

I like you.
Jeg kan lide dig.
yie kan lee die

I love you.
Jeg elsker dig.
yie <u>ehl</u>-skah die

THE DATING GAME

Would you like to go out...?	**Kunne du tænke dig at gå ud...?** *koon • ner doo tehnker die at gaw oodh*
for coffee	**og få en kop kaffe** *ow fow ehn kop kaf • eh*
for a drink	**og få en drink** *ow fow ehn drienk*
to dinner	**spise middag** *spee • ser mid • da*
What are your plans for...?	**Hvad er dine planer for...?** *vadh ehr dee • ner pla • nah foh...*
today	**i dag** *ee da*
tonight	**i aften** *ee <u>ahf</u> • tern*
tomorrow	**i morgen** *ee m<u>oh</u>n*
this weekend	**weekenden** *v<u>ee</u> • gehn • dern*
Where would you like to go?	**Hvor har du lyst til at gå hen?** *voar hah doo lurst til ad gow hehn*
I'd like to go to...	**Jeg vil gerne...** *yie vil <u>gehr</u> • ner...*

Do you like...?	**Har du lyst til at...?**
	hah doo lurst til ad...
Can I have your number/e-mail?	**Må jeg få dit nummer/din e-mail adresse?**
	mow yie fow deet noa • mah/deen ee • mayl • a • drah • ser
Are you on Facebook /Twitter?	**Er du på Facebook/Twitter?**
	ehr doo paw Facebook/Twitter
Can I join you?	**Må jeg komme med dig?**
	mow yie koh • mer mehdh die
You're very attractive.	**Du er meget køn.**
	doo ehr mie • erdh kurn
Shall we go somewhere quieter?	**Skal vi gå hen et sted, hvor der er mere stille?**
	skal vee gow hen eht stehdh voar dehr ehr meh • ah sti • ler

For Communications, see page 84.

ACCEPTING & REJECTING

Thanks, I'd love to.	**Tak, det vil jeg meget gerne.**
	tahk deh vil yie mie • erdh gehr • ner
Where can we meet?	**Hvor skal vi mødes?**
	voar skal vee mur • dhers
I'll meet you at the bar/your hotel.	**Jeg møder dig i baren/på dit hotel.**
	yie mur•dhah die ee bahn/paw deet hoa • tehl
I'll come by at...	**Jeg kommer klokken...**
	yie koh • mah kloh • gehrn...
What's your address?	**Hvad er din adresse?**
	vadh ehr deen a • drah • ser
Thank you, but I'm busy.	**Tak, men jeg er desværre optaget.**
	tahk mehn yie ehr deh • svehr ohp • ta • erdh

No thanks, I'm not interested. **Nej tak, jeg er ikke interesseret.**
nie tahk yie ehr ig • ger in • trah • seh • erdh

Leave me alone! **Vær rar og lad mig være i fred!**
vehr rah ow la mie vay • er ee frehdh

Stop bothering me! **Lad mig være i fred!**
la mie vay•er ee frehdh

For Time, see page 23.

GETTING INTIMATE

Can I hug/kiss you? **Må jeg kramme/kysse dig?**
mow yie krah • mer/kur • ser die

Yes. **Ja.**
ya

No. **Nej.**
nie

Stop! **Stop!**
Stohb

SEXUAL PREFERENCES

Are you gay? **Er du homoseksuel?**
ehr doo hoa • moa • sehk • soo • ehl

I'm... **Jeg er...**
yie ehr...

heterosexual **heteroseksuel**
heh • teh • roa • sehk • soo • ehl

homosexual **homoseksuel**
hoa • moa • sehk • soo • ehl

bisexual **biseksuel**
bee • sehk • soo • ehl

Do you like men/women? **Er du til mænd/kvinder?**
ehr doo til mehn/kveen • ar

hviilet b...

Den i Livet velær...

Herr JACOB...

Sögne Præst for Swerborg M

Föd den 19 Februa...

Kaldet til Præste embede

indgick i ægtestand med

Dÿdædle Matron...

død den 29

En Mand i sit Kald af

at hans fodspor ikk...

I sit hiius af saad...

...af eu efterladt

...til sidste

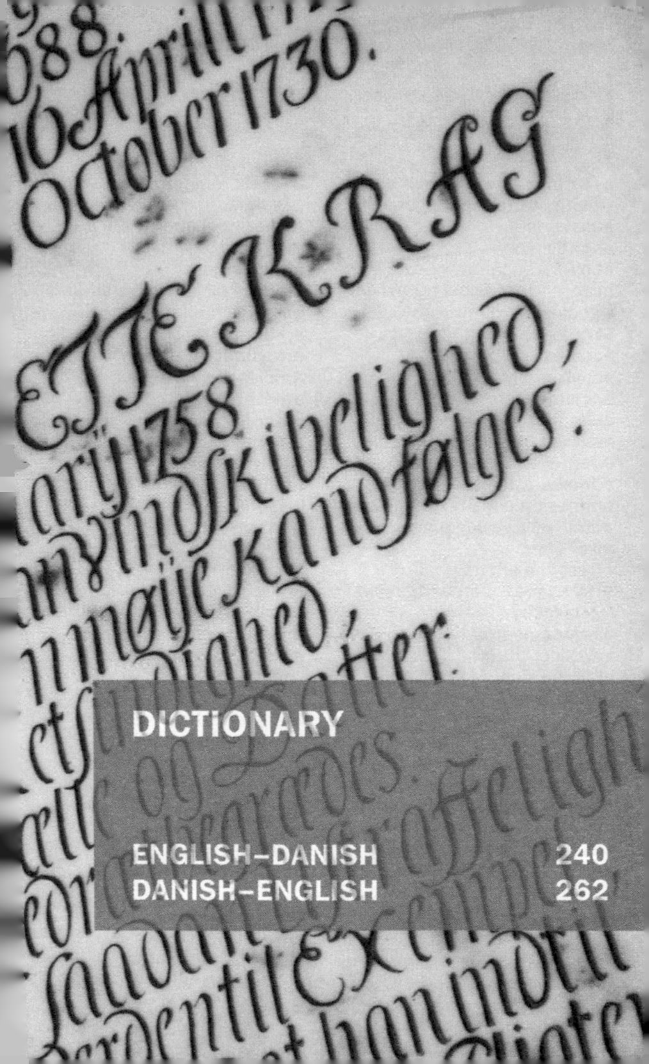

DICTIONARY

ENGLISH–DANISH

A

a (with common nouns) en; **(with neuter nouns)** et
able kunne
about cirka
above ovenpå
accept v tage imod; **(approval)** godkende
access n adgang
accessory tilbehør
accident ulykke
account konto
ache smerte
acupuncture akupunktur
adapter adapter
address n adresse
admission adgang
admitted give adgang for
after efter
afternoon eftermiddag
aftershave lotion barbersprit
again igen
against mod
age alder
air conditioning klimaanlæg
air mattress luftmadras
airmail luftpost
airplane fly
airport lufthavn
aisle seat sæde ved midtergangen
alarm clock vækkeur
alcohol alkohol
alcoholic adj alkoholisk

allergic allergisk
allergic reaction allergisk reaktion
alphabet alfabet
also også
alter v ændre
altitude sickness bjergsyge
amazing forbløffende
amber rav
ambulance ambulance
American amerikaner
amethyst ametyst
amount n **(money)** beløb
amusement park forlystelsespark
analgesic smertestillende middel
and og
anesthetic narkose
animal dyr
ankle ankel
answer svar
antibiotic antibiotikum
antidepressant antidepressivt middel
antique antikvitet
antiques store antikvitetshandler
antiseptic cream antiseptisk creme
any nogen
anyone nogen
anything noget
anywhere hvor som helst

---

adj adjective	**BE** British English	**prep** preposition
adv adverb	**n** noun	**v** verb

apartment lejlighed
aperitif aperitif
appendix blindtarm
appliance udstyr
appointment aftale
arcade spillehal
architect arkitekt
arm arm
aromatherapy aromaterapi
around (approximately)
omkring; (around the corner)
rundt om
arrival ankomst
arrive ankomme
art kunst
art gallery kunstgalleri
aspirin hovedpinepille
assistance hjælp
assorted blandet
asthma astma
astringent sammentrækkende
middel
at ved
ATM pengeautomat
attack n overfald
attend deltage
attractive køn
audio guide lydguide
Australia Australien
average gennemsnitlig
away væk
awful skrækkelig

B
baby baby
baby bottle sutteflaske
baby food babymad
baby wipes vådservietter
babysitter babysitter
back ryg
backache rygsmerter
backpack rygsæk
bad dårlig

bag (purse) taske; (shopping)
pose
baggage [BE] bagage
baggage check
bagageopbevaring
baggage claim bagagebånd
bakery bageri
balance (finance) saldo
balcony altan
ballet ballet
bandage n plaster
bank (finance) bank
bank note seddel
bar bar
barber herrefrisør
basket kurv
basketball game
basketballkamp
bath bad
bathing suit badedragt
bathrobe badekåbe
bathroom badeværelse
battery batteri
battleground kampplads
be være
beach ball badebold
beard skæg
beautiful smuk
beauty salon skønhedssalon
bed seng
before (time) før
begin begynde
behind bagved
beige beige
bell (electric) ringeklokke
below nedenunder
belt bælte
berth køje
better bedre
between mellem
bicycle cykel
big stor
bike route cykelsti

bikini bikini
bill (restaurant) regning; **(bank note)** seddel
binoculars kikkert
bird fugl
birth fødsel
birthday fødselsdag
black sort
bladder blære
blade barberblad
blanket tæppe
bleach blegning
bleed bløde
blind (window) rullegardin
blister blist
blocked stoppet
blood blod
blood pressure blodtryk
blouse bluse
blow dry føntørre
blue blå
boat båd
boat trip bådtur
body krop
bone knogle
book bog
booklet (of tickets) rabatkort
bookstore boghandel
boot støvle
boring kedelig
born født
botanical garden botanisk have
botany botanik
bother genere
bottle flaske
bottle opener oplukker
bottom forneden
bowel tarm
bowl skål
box æske
boxing match boksekamp
boy dreng
boyfriend kæreste

bra bh
bracelet armbånd
brake n bremse
break (out of order) være i uorden
breakdown (car) få motorstop
breakfast morgenmad
breast bryst
breathe trække vejret
bridge bro
bring tage med
bring down få ned
British (person) brite; adj britisk
broken i stykker
brooch broche
broom kost
brown brun
bruise blåt mærke
brush n børste
bucket spand
bug insekt
build bygge
building bygning
burn brandsår
bus bus
bus station busstation
bus stop busholdeplads
business card visitkort
business center (at hotel) businesscenter
business class business class
business district forretningskvarter
business trip forretningsrejse
busy optaget
but men
butane gas flaskegas
butcher slagter
button knap
buy købe

C

cabin (ship) kahyt
cafe café

calculator regnemaskine
calendar kalender
call n (phone) opringning; v
  ringe; (summon) ringe efter
calm rolig
camera kamera
camera case fototaske
camera shop fotoforretning
camp bed campingseng
camp v campere
camping camping
camping equipment
  campingudstyr
campsite campingplads
can opener dåseåbner
can v (be able to) kan; n
  (container) dåse
Canada Canada
Canadian canadier
cancel annullere
candle stearinlys
candy store slikbutik
cap kasket
car bil
car hire [BE] biludlejning
car mechanic bilmekaniker
car park [BE] parkeringsplads
car rental biludlejning
car seat barnesæde
carafe karaffel
card kort
card game kortspil
cardigan cardigan
carry bære
cart indkøbsvogn
carton (of cigarettes) karton
case (camera) taske
cash v indløse; n kontant
cashier kasse
casino kasino
castle slot; borg
caution forsigtig
cave hule

CD cd
cell phone mobiltelefon
cemetery kirkegård
center of town centrum
centimeter centimeter
ceramics keramik
certain vis
certificate attest
chair stol
change n (money) byttepenge;
  v (money) veksle; v (clothes,
  diaper) skifte
charcoal trækul
charge n gebyr; v koste
cheap billig
check (restaurant) n regning;
  (banking) check; v (someone,
  something) kontrollere;
  (luggage) tjekke ind
check-in desk (airport) check-in
  skranke
checking account checkkonto
check out v tjekke ud
check-up (medical)
  undersøgelse
cheers skål
chef køkkenchef
chemical toilet kemisk toilet
chemist [BE] apotek
cheque [BE] check
chess skak
chess set skakspil
chest brystkasse
chest pain smerter i brystet
child barn
child's seat barnesæde
children's clothing børnetøj
children's portion børneportion
choice valg
church kirke
cigar cigar
cigarette cigaret
cinema [BE] biograf

classical klassisk
clean *adj* ren; *v* gøre rent
cleansing cream rensecreme
clear *v* slette
cliff klippe
clip clips
clock ur
close *v* lukke
closed lukket
cloth stof
clothing tøj
clothing store tøjbutik
cloud sky
coat *n* (clothing) frakke
coin mønt
cold (illness) forkølelse; *adj* kold
collar flip
colleague kollega
color farve
comb kam
come komme
comedy lystspil
commission (fee) kommission
common (frequent) almindelig
compartment (train) kupé
compass kompas
complaint klage
computer computer; pc
concert koncert
concert hall koncertsal
condom kondom
conference room mødelokale
confirm bekræfte
confirmation bekræftelse
congratulations til lykke
connect *v* koble sig på
connection (transportation, internet) forbindelse
constipation forstoppelse
consulate konsulat
contact lens kontaktlinse
contagious smitsom
contain indeholde

contraceptive præventivmiddel
contract kontrakt
control kontrol
convention hall konferencesal
cooking facilities køkkenfaciliteter
copper kobber
corkscrew proptrækker
corner hjørne
cost *n* omkostning; *v* koste
cot klapseng
cotton bomuld
cough *n* hoste
counter disk
country land
countryside på landet
court house retsbygning
cover charge beregning per kuvert
cramps krampe
crayon farveblyant
cream (toiletry) creme
credit kredit
credit card kreditkort
crib barneseng
crockery [BE] spisestel
cross-country skiing langrend
crossing (maritime) overfart
crossroads vejkryds
crown (Danish currency) krone
crystal krystal
cufflink manchetknap
cuisine køkken
cup kop
currency valuta
currency exchange office vekselkontor
current (ocean) strøm
curtain gardin
customs told
customs declaration form toldangivelsesformular
cut *n* (wound) snitsår; *v* (with

scissors) klippe
cut glass slebet glas
cycling race cykelløb

D

dairy mejeri
damaged beskadiget
dance club diskotek
dance *n* dans; *v* danse
danger fare
dangerous farlig
Danish (person) dansker; *adj* dansk
dark mørk
date (appointment) stævnemøde; **(day)** dato
day dag
decision beslutning
deck (ship) dæk
deck chair liggestol
declare (customs) fortolde
deep dyb
degree (temperature) grad
delay forsinkelse
delicatessen delikatesseforretning
delicious dejlig
deliver levere
delivery levering
denim denim
Denmark Danmark
dentist tandlæge
denture protese
deodorant deodorant
depart afgå
department (shop) afdeling
department store stormagasin
departure afgang
departure gate afgangsgate
deposit *n* **(bank)** indskud; **(down payment)** depositum
dessert dessert
detergent opvaskemiddel

detour (traffic) omkørsel
diabetic diabetiker
diamond diamant
diaper ble
diarrhea diarré
dictionary ordbog
diesel diesel
diet kost
difficult svær
digital digital
dining car spisevogn
dining room spisesalen
dinner middag

direct *adj* direkte; *v* **(someone)** vise vej til
direction vejangivelse
directory (phone) telefonbog
dirty beskidt
disabled handicappet
disc (parking) parkeringsskive
disconnect *v* **(computer)** koble sig fra
discount rabat
disease sygdom
dish (food item) ret
dishes (plates) spisetallerkner
dishwasher opvaskemaskine
dishwashing detergent opvaskemiddel
disinfectant desinficeringsmiddel
display case udstillingsmontre
district (of town) kvarter
disturb forstyrre
divorced skilt
dizzy svimmel
doctor læge
doctor's office lægekonsultation
dog hund
doll dukke
dollar (U.S.) dollar

domestic (airport terminal) indenrigs
domestic flight indenrigsfly
double bed dobbeltseng
double room dobbeltværelse
down ned
downtown area indre by
dozen dusin
dress n kjole
drink n drikkevare; **(cocktail)** drink; v drikke
drinking water drikkevand
drip dryppe
drive køre
driver's license kørekort
drop (liquid) dråbe
drugstore apotek
dry tør
dry cleaner renseri
dummy [BE] (baby's) sut
during i løbet af
duty (customs) told
duty-free goods toldfri varer
duty-free shop toldfri butik
dye farvning

E

each hver
ear øre
ear drops øredråber
earache ondt i ørerne
early tidligt
earring ørenring
east øst
easy nem
eat spise
economy class økonomiklasse
elastic elastik
electric elektrisk
electrical outlet stikkontakt
electricity elektricitet
electronic elektronisk
elevator elevator

e-mail e-mail
e-mail address e-mail-adresse
embassy ambassade
embroidery broderi
emerald smaragd
emergency nødstilfælde
emergency exit nødudgang
empty tom
enamel emalje
end slutning
engaged (phone) optaget
England England
English (language) engelsk; **(person)** englænder
enjoyable dejlig
enlarge forstørre
enough nok
enter v indtaste
entrance indgang
entrance fee entré
entry (access) adgang
envelope konvolut
equipment udstyr
eraser viskelæder
escalator rulletrappe
estimate n overslag; **(quotation)** tilbud
e-ticket e-billet
e-ticket check-in e-billet check-in
eurocheque eurocheck
Europe Europa
European Union Europæiske Fællesskab
evening aften
every hver
everything alt
exchange rate vekselkurs
exchange v **(money)** veksle
excursion udflugt
excuse v undskylde
exhibition udstilling
exit n udgang; v **(computer)** forlade

expect vente
expense udgift
expensive dyr
express ekspres
expression udtryk
extension (phone) lokal
extra ekstra
eye øje
eye drops øjendråber
eye shadow øjenskygge
eyesight syn

F
fabric (cloth) stof
face ansigt
facial ansigtsbehandling
factory fabrik
fair messe
fall v falde
family familie
fan ventilator
far langt
fare (ticket) billet
farm bondegård
far-sighted langsynet
fast adj hurtig
fast-food place burgerbar
faucet vandhane
fax fax
fax number faxnummer
fee (commission) kommission
feed v made
feel (physical state) føle
ferry færge
fever feber
few et par stykker
field mark
file (for nails) fil
fill in (form) udfylde
filling (tooth) plombe
film [BE] film
filter filter
find v finde

fine (OK) fint
fine arts kunst
finger finger
fire brand
fire door branddør
fire escape brandtrappe
fire exit nødudgang
first første
first-aid kit nødhjælpskasse
first class første klasse
first course forret
fishing fiskeri
fit v passe
fitting room prøverum
fix v reparere
flashlight lommelygte
flat [BE] (apartment) lejlighed
flatware bestik
flea market loppemarked
flight fly
floor etage
florist blomsterhandler
flower blomst
flu influenza
fluid væske
fog tåge
follow følge
food mad
food poisoning madforgiftning
foot fod
football [BE] fodbold
for for
forbidden forbudt
forecast vejrudsigt
foreign udenlandsk
forest skov
forget glemme
fork gaffel
form (document) formular
fountain springvand
frame (glasses) stel
free ledigt
freezer fryser

fresh frisk
friend ven
from fra
frost frostvejr
frying pan stegepande
full fuld
full-time fuldtids
furniture møbel

G

gallery galleri
game spil
garage garage
garbage skrald
garden have
gas benzin
gasoline benzin
gauze gaze
gem ædelsten
general almindelig
general delivery poste restante
general practitioner [BE]
  praktiserende læge
genuine ægte
get (find) komme til
get off stige af
get up stå op
gift gave
gift shop gavebutik
girl pige
girlfriend kæreste
give give
gland kirtel
glass (drinking) glas
glasses (optical) briller
glove handske
glue lim
go away gå væk
go back køre tilbage
go out gå ud
gold guld
golf club golfkølle
golf course golfbane

golf tournament golfturnering
good god
good afternoon goddag
good evening godaften
good morning godmorgen
good night godnat
goodbye farvel
gram gram
grandchild barnebarn
gray grå
great (excellent) storartet
Great Britain Storbritannien
green grøn
greengrocer's [BE] grønthandler
greeting hilsen
ground-floor room [BE] værelse
  i stueetagen
groundsheet teltunderlag
group gruppe
guesthouse pensionat
guide dog førerhund
guide n guide
guidebook rejsefører
gym motionscenter
gynecologist gynækolog

H

hair hår
hair dryer hårtørrer
hairbrush hårbørste
haircut klipning
hairdresser frisør
hairspray hårlak
hall (room) sal
hammer hammer
hammock hængekøje
hand hånd
hand cream håndcreme
hand washable vaske i hånden
handbag [BE] håndtaske
handicrafts kunsthåndværk
handkerchief lommetørklæde
handmade håndlavet

hanger bøjle
happy glad
harbor havn
hard hård
hardware store isenkræmmer
hare hare
hat hat
have (must) skulle; **(possess)** have
hay fever høfeber
head hoved
headache hovedpine
headlight billygte
headphones hovedtelefon
health food store helsekostforretning
health insurance sygeforsikring
hearing-impaired hørehæmmet
heart hjerte
heart attack hjerteanfald
heat v opvarme
heating varme
heavy tung
hello hej
helmet hjelm
help hjælp; **(oneself)** tage selv
here her
hi hej
high adj høj
high tide flod
highchair høj stol
highway motorvej
hill bakke
hire [BE] v leje
history historie
hole hul
holiday helligdag; **[BE]** ferie
home hjem
horseback riding ridning
hospital hospital
hot (temperature) varm
hotel hotel
hotel directory hotelfortegnelse

hotel reservation værelsesbestilling
hour (time) time
house hus
how hvordan
how far hvor langt
how long hvor længe
how many hvor mange
how much hvor meget
hug v kramme
hungry sulten
hunting jagt
hurry travlt
hurt gøre ondt
husband mand

I

I jeg
ice is
icy (weather) iskoldt
identification (card) id-kort
if hvis
ill [BE] syg
illness sygdom
important vigtig
imported importeret
impressive imponerende
in i
include iberegne
indoor indendørs
inexpensive billig
infected betændt
infection betændelse
inflammation betændelse
information information
information desk informationsluge
injection indsprøjtning
injure komme til skade
injury kvæstelse
inn kro
innocent uskyldig
inquiry forespørgsel

insect bite insektbid
insect repellent insekt-spray
insect spray insekt-spray
inside indenfor
instant messenger instant
    messenger
insurance forsikring
insurance claim forsikringskrav
interest (finance) rente
interested interesseret
interesting interessant
international international;
    (airport terminal) udenrigs
international flight udenrigsfly
internet internet
internet cafe internetcafé
interpreter tolk
intersection vejkryds
introduce præsentere
introduction (social)
    præsentation
investment investering
invitation indbydelse
invite v indbyde
invoice faktura
iodine jod
Ireland Irland
Irish (person) irlænder, adj irsk
iron n (clothing) strygejern; v
    stryge
itemized bill udspecificeret
    regning

J
jacket jakke
jar (container) glas
jaw kæbe
jazz jazz
jeans cowboybukser
jet ski jetski
jeweler guldsmed
join v komme med
joint (anatomy) led

journey rejse
just (only) bare

K
keep beholde
kerosene petroleum
key nøgle
key card nøglekort
kiddie pool børnebassin
kidney nyre
kilogram kilogram
kilometer kilometer
kind adj rar; n slags
kiss v kysse
knee knæ
knife kniv
knitwear strikvarer
knock banke på
know vide

L
label etiket
lace blonde
lactose intolerant
    laktoseintolerant
lake sø
lamp lampe
landscape landskab
language sprog
lantern lygte
large stor
last sidst
late (time) sent; (delay)
    forsinket
laugh grine
launderette [BE] møntvaskeri
laundromat møntvaskeri
laundry vasketøj
laundry facilities vaskerum
laundry service vaskeri
lawyer advokat
laxative afføringsmiddel
leather læder

leave *v* afgå; **(behind)** efterlade
left til venstre
left-luggage office **[BE]**
  bagageopbevaring
leg ben
lens **(camera)** objektiv;
  (glasses) linse
less mindre
lesson undervisning
letter brev
library bibliotek
license **(driving)** kørekort
life boat redningsbåd
life guard **(beach)** livredder
life jacket redningsvest
life preserver redningsbælte
lift **[BE]** elevator
light **(color)** lys; **(weight)** let
light bulb pære
lighter lighter
lightning lyn
like vil gerne; **(please)** kan lide
linen lærred
lip læbe
lipstick læbestift
liquor store vinhandel
listen høre på
liter liter
little **(amount)** en smule
live *v* bo
loafers hyttesko
local lokal
log off logge af
log on logge på
login log ind
long lange
long-sighted **[BE]** langsynet
look *v* se
lose miste
loss tab
lost faret vild
lost and found hittegodskontor
lost property office **[BE]**

hittegodskontor
lotion lotion
loud **(voice)** høj
love *v* elske
lovely dejlig
low lav
low tide ebbe
luck lykke
luggage bagage
luggage cart bagagevogn
luggage locker bagageboks
lunch frokost
lung lunge

M

magazine blad
magnificent storartet
maid stuepige
mail *n* post; *v* poste
mailbox postkasse
make-up *n* sminke
mall butikscenter
mallet kølle
man mand
manager direktør
manicure manicure
many mange
map kort
market *n* market
married gift
mass **(religious service)** messe
massage massage
match *n* **(sport)** kamp
material stof
matinée eftermiddagsforestilling
mattress madras
may *v* må
meadow eng
meal måltid
mean *v* betyde
measure tage mål af
measuring cup målekrus
measuring spoon måleske

mechanic mekaniker
medicine (drug) medicin
meet mødes
memorial mindesmærke
memory card hukommelseskort
mend reparere
menu menu; menukort
message besked
meter meter
middle midten
midnight midnat
mileage kilometerpenge
minute minut
mirror spejl
miscellaneous forskellig
Miss frøken
miss v **(lacking)** mangle
mistake fejltagelse
mobile phone [BE] mobiltelefon
moisturizing cream
  fugtighedscreme
moment øjeblik
money penge
money order postanvisning
month måned
monument monument
moon måne
mop n moppe
moped knallert
more mere
morning morgen
mosque moské
mosquito net myggenet
motel motel
motorboat motorbåd
motorcycle motorcykel
motorway [BE] motorvej
moustache overskæg
mouth mund
mouthwash mundvand
move v flytte
movie film
Mr. hr.

Mrs. fru
much meget
mug n krus
mugging overfald
muscle muskel
museum museum
music musik
musical musical
must (have to) måtte

N

nail (body) negl
nail clippers negleklipper
nail file neglefil
nail salon neglesalon
name navn
napkin serviet
nappy [BE] ble
narrow smal
nationality nationalitet
natural naturlig
nausea kvalme
near nær
nearby i nærheden
near-sighted nærsynet
neck hals
necklace halskæde
need v brug for
needle nål
nerve nerve
never aldrig
new ny
newspaper avis
newsstand aviskiosk
next næste
next to ved siden af
nice (beautiful) dejlig
night nat
no nej
noisy støjende
none ingen
non-smoking ikke-ryger
noon middag

normal normal
north nord
nose næse
not ikke
note (bank note) seddel
notebook notesbog
nothing ikke noget
notice (sign) skilt
notify underrette
novice begynderniveau
now nu
number nummer
nurse sygeplejerske

O

o'clock klokken
occupation stilling
occupied optaget
office kontor
off-licence [BE] vinhandel
oil spiseolie
old gammel
old town gamle bydel
on på
on time til tiden
once en gang
one-way ticket enkeltbillet
only kun
open adj åben; v åbne
opera opera
operation operation
operator telefonist
opposite overfor
optician optiker
or eller
orange (color) orange
orchestra orkester; (seats)
  parket
order n bestilling; v bestille
out of order virker ikke
out of stock udsolgt
outlet (electric) stikkontakt
outside udenfor

oval oval
overlook n udkigspost
oxygen treatment
  oxygenbehandling

P

pacifier (baby's) sut
packet pakke
pad (sanitary) hygiejnebind
pail spand
pain smerte
painkiller smertestillende
  middel
paint n maling; v male
painting maleri
pair par
pajamas pyjamas
palace slot
palpitations hjertebanken
pants bukser
panty hose strømpebukser
paper papir
paper towel papirhåndklæde
parcel [BE] pakke
parents forældre
park n park; v parkere
parking parkering
parking disc parkeringsskive
parking garage
  parkeringskælder
parking lot parkeringsplads
parking meter parkometer
part del
part-time deltid
party (social gathering) fest
passport pas
passport control paskontrol
passport photo pasfoto
paste (glue) klister
pastry shop konditori
patch lappe
path sti
patient patient

pattern mønster
pay betale
payment betaling
peak n (mountain) bjergtop
pearl perle
pedestrian fodgænger
pediatrician børnelæge
pedicure pedicure
peg (tent) pløk
pen pen; kuglepen
pencil blyant
pendant vedhæng
penicillin penicillin
per day per dag
per hour per time
per person per person
per week per uge
percentage procentsats
perfume parfume
perhaps måske
period (monthly) menstruation
permit n (fishing) fiskekort;
  (hunting) jagtkort
person person
personal personlig
petite petit
petrol [BE] benzin
pewter tinlegering
pharmacy apotek
phone card telefonkort
photo billede
photocopy n fotokopi
photograph n billede
photography fotografering
phrase vending
pick up v (go get) hente
picnic medbragt mad
picnic basket madkurv
piece stykke
pill pille
pillow pude
PIN pinkode
pin n (brooch) nål

pink lyserød
pipe pibe
place n sted
plane fly
planetarium planetarium
plaster [BE] (bandage) plaster
plastic plastic
plastic bag plasticpose
plastic wrap plastikfolie
plate tallerken
platform [BE] (station) perron
platinum platin
play n (theatre) stykke; v spille
playground legeplads
playpen kravlegård
please vær venlig
plug (electric) stik
plunger svuppert; vaskesuger
pneumonia lungebetændelse
pocket lomme
point of interest seværdighed
point v pege
poison gift
poisoning forgiftning
pole (ski) skistav; (tent)
  teltstang
police politi
police report politianmeldelse
police station politistation
pond dam
pool svømmebassin
porcelain porcelæn
port havn
portable transportabel
porter portier
portion portion
post [BE] n post; v poste
post office posthus
postage porto
postage stamp frimærke
postcard postkort
pot gryde
pottery pottemageri

pound (British currency, weight) pund
powder pudder
pregnant gravid
premium (gas) 98 oktan
prescribe skrive recept på
prescription recept
present n gave
press (iron) presse
pressure tryk
pretty køn
price pris
price-fixed menu dagens menu
print n (photo) aftryk; v (document) udskrive
private privat
profit n overskud
program (of events) program
pronounce v udtale
pronunciation n udtale
provide skaffe
pull v trække
pump pumpe
puncture punktering
purchase n køb; v købe
pure ren
purple violet
purse (handbag) håndtaske
push v skubbe
pushchair [BE] klapvogn
put sætte

Q

quality kvalitet
quantity mængde
question n spørgsmål
quick hurtig
quiet stille

R

race væddeløb
race track væddeløbsbane
racket (sport) ketsjer

radio radio
railway station [BE] jernbanestation
rain regnvejr
raincoat regnfrakke
rape n voldtægt
rash udslet
rate n (exchange) vekselkurs; (price) takst
razor barbermaskine
razor blade barberblad
ready færdig
real (genuine) ægte
rear bagerst
receipt kvittering
reception reception
receptionist receptionist
recommend anbefale
rectangular rektangulær
red rød
reduction rabat
refrigerator køleskab
refund v få pengene tilbage
regards hilsner
region område
registered mail anbefalet
registration indskrivning
regular (gas) 95 oktan
relationship forhold
reliable pålidelig
religion religion
rent v leje
rental udlejning
rental car udlejningsbil
repair n reparation; v reparere
repeat v gentage
report (theft) anmelde
request n anmodning; v anmode
required nødvendig
requirement forespørgsel
reservation reservation
reservations office pladsreserveringen

reserve bestille
reserved reserveret
rest n rest
restaurant restaurant
restroom toilet
retired pensioneret
return (come back) komme
tilbage; (give back) returnere
return ticket [BE] returbillet
rib ribben
ribbon bånd
right (correct) rigtigt; (direction)
til højre
ring (jewelry) ring; (bell) ringe
på
river flod
road vej
road assistance hjælp på vejen
road map vejkort
road sign vejskilt
robbery tyveri
romantic romantisk
room (hotel) værelse; (space)
plads
room number værelsesnummer
room service roomservice;
service på værelset
room temperature
rumtemperatur
rope reb
round rund
round (golf) runde
round-trip ticket returbillet
route rute
rowboat robåd
rubber (material) gummi
rubbish [BE] skrald
ruby rubin

S

safe n (vault) boks; (not in
danger) sikker
safety pin sikkerhedsnål

sailboat sejlbåd
sale n salg; (bargains) udsalg
same samme
sand sand
sandal sandal
sanitary napkin hygiejnebind
sapphire safir
satin satin
saucepan kasserolle
saucer underkop
sauna sauna
save v gemme
savings account
opsparingskonto
scarf tørklæde
scenery landskab
scenic route køn rute
school skole
scissors saks
scooter scooter
Scotland Skotland
screwdriver skruetrækker
sculpture skulptur
sea hav
season sæson
seat plads
seat belt sele
second sekund
second class anden klasse
second-hand shop
marskandiser; genbrugsbutik
section afdeling
see se
sell sælge
send sende
senior citizen pensionist
sentence sætning
separated (relationship)
separeret
serious alvorlig
serve (meal) servere
service (restaurant) betjening
set menu fast menu

sew sy
shampoo shampoo
shape form
sharp (pain) skarp
shave n barbering
shaving brush barberbørste
shaving cream barbercreme
shelf hylde
ship n skib; v forsende
shirt skjorte
shoe sko
shoe store skoforretning
shop n butik
shopping indkøb
shopping area indkøbscenter
shopping centre [BE]
  butikscenter
shopping mall butikscenter
short kort
shorts shorts
short-sighted [BE] kortsynet
shoulder skulder
shovel n skovl
show n show; v vise
shower (stall) bruser
shrine helgengrav
shut lukket
shutter (window) skodde
side side
sightseeing sightseeing
sightseeing tour rundtur
sign underskrive
sign (notice) skilt;
  v underskrive
signature underskrift
silk silke
silver sølv
silverware sølvtøj
since siden
sing synge
single n (ticket) enkeltbillet;
  (unmarried) ugift
single room enkeltværelse

size størrelse; (clothes) mål;
  (shoes) nummer
skate v skøjte
skating rink skøjtebane
skin hud
skirt nederdel
sky himmel
sleep v sove
sleeping bag sovepose
sleeping car sovevogn
sleeping pill sovepille
sleeve ærme
slice n skive
slide (photo) dias
slipper hjemmesko
slow langsom
small lille
smoke ryge
smoker ryger
snack mellemmåltid
snack bar snackbar
sneaker gummisko
snorkeling equipment
  snorkeludstyr
snow sne
soap sæbe
soccer fodbold
soccer match fodboldkamp
sock sok
socket (electric) stikkontakt
soft blød
sold out udsolgt
someone nogen
something noget
song sang
soon snart
sore (painful) øm
sore throat ondt i halsen
sorry beklager
sort (kind) slags
south syd
souvenir souvenir
souvenir shop souvenirbutik

spa spa
spatula spatel
speak v tale
special særlig
specialist specialist
speciality specialitet
spell v stave
spend bruge
spine rygrad
sponge svamp
spoon ske
sport sport
sporting goods store sportsforretning
sprained forstuvet
square (shape) firkantet
stadium stadium
staff personale
stain plet
stainless steel rustfrit stål
stairs trappe
stamp n (postage) frimærke; v (ticket) stemple
staple hæfteklamme
star stjerne
start begynde
starter [BE] (meal) forret
station (train) jernbanestation; (subway) S-togsstation
stationery store papirhandel
stay (trip) ophold; v (remain) blive; v (reside) bo
steal stjæle
sterling silver sterlingsølv
sting n stik; v stikke
stockings strømpe
stomach mave
stomachache mavepine
stop (bus) busholdeplads; v stop
store (shop) forretning
store directory butiksoversigt
stove ovn
straight ahead ligeud

strange underlig
street gade
street map gadekort
string snor
stroller klapvogn
strong stærk
student studerende
study v studere
stunning fantastisk flot
sturdy solid
subway metro
subway map togkort
suit (man's) habit; (woman's) dragt
suitcase kuffert
sun sol
sunburn solforbrænding
sunglasses solbriller
sunstroke solstik
sun-tan lotion solcreme
super (gas) 98 oktan
supermarket supermarked
supplement n tillæg
suppository stikpille
surgery [BE] lægekonsultation
surname efternavn
swallow sluge
sweater sweater
sweatshirt sweatshirt
sweet sød
swell hæve
swelling hævelse
swim v svømme
swimming svømning
swimming pool svømmebasin
swimming trunks badebukser
swollen hævet
symbol symbol
synagogue synagoge
synthetic syntetisk
system system

T

table bord
tablet (medical) pille
tailor skrædder
take tage
take away v [BE] tage med
taken (occupied) taget
tampon tampon
tap (water) vandhane
tax skat
taxi taxa
taxi rank [BE] taxaholdeplads
taxi stand taxaholdeplads
team hold
tear v rive i stykker
teaspoon teske
telephone booth telefonboks
telephone directory telefonbog
telephone n telefon; v ringe
telephone number
  telefonnummer
tell sige
temperature temperatur
temple tempel
temporary midlertidig
tennis court tennisbane
tennis match tenniskamp
tennis racket tennisketsjer
tent telt
tent peg teltpløk
tent pole teltstang
terminal terminal
terrace terrasse
terrible frygtelig
terrifying skrækindjagende
thank takke
thank you tak
theater teater
theft tyveri
then så
there der
thermometer termometer
thief tyv

thigh lår
thin tynd
think (believe) tro
thirsty tørstig
thread tråd
throat hals
through gennem
thumb tommelfinger
thunder torden
thunderstorm tordenvejr
ticket billet
ticket office billetluge
tide ebbe
tie slips
tie clip slipseklemme
time n tid; (recurrent occasion)
  gang
timetable [BE] køreplan
tin [BE] (container) dåse
tin opener [BE] dåseåbner
tire dæk
tired træt
tissue papirslommetørklæde
to til
tobacco tobak
tobacconist tobakshandler
today i dag
toe tå
toilet [BE] toilet
toilet paper toiletpapir
toiletry toiletartikel
tomb gravsted
tomorrow i morgen
tongue tunge
tonight i aften
too (also) også
too much for meget
tool værktøj
tooth tand
toothache tandpine
toothbrush tandbørste
toothpaste tandpasta
torn (clothes) gået i stykker

touch v røre
tour tur
tourist office turistkontor
tow truck kranbil
towards mod
towel håndklæde
tower tårn
town by
town hall rådhus
toy legetøj
toy store legetøjsforretning
track (train) spor
traffic light trafiklys
trail gangsti
trailer campingvogn
train tog
tram sporvogn
tranquillizer beroligende middel
transfer (money) overførsel
translate oversætte
travel rejse
travel agency rejsebureau
travel guide rejsefører
travel sickness køresyge
traveler's check rejsecheck
treatment behandling
tree træ
trim studsning
trip rejse
trolley bagagevogn
trousers [BE] bukser
T-shirt T-shirt
tube tube
turn (change direction) drej til
turtleneck højhalset
TV fjernsyn
tweezers pincet

U

ugly grim
umbrella paraply; (beach)
  parasol
unconscious bevidstløs

under under
underground station [BE]
  metrostation
underpants underbukser
undershirt undertrøje
understand forstå
undress tage tøjet af
United States USA
university universitet
unleaded (fuel) blyfri
until indtil
up op
upstairs ovenpå
urgent haster
use brug
usually normalt

V

vacancy ledigt værelse
vacant ledig
vacation ferie
vaccinate vaccinere
vacuum cleaner støvsuger
valley dal
value værdi
value-added tax [BE] moms
vegetarian vegetar
vein vene
very meget
veterinarian dyrlæge
video camera videokamera
view (panorama) udsigt
village landsby
visit n besøg; v besøge
visiting hours besøgstid
visually impaired synshæmmet
V-neck V-hals
volleyball game volleyballkamp
voltage spænding
vomit v kaste op

W

wait v vente

waiter tjener
waiting room venteværelse
waitress kvindelig tjener
wake vække
wake-up call morgenvækning
Wales Wales
walk n gåtur
wall mur
wallet tegnebog
want vil have
warm (temperature) varm; v
   (reheat) opvarme
wash vaske
washing machine
   vaskemaskine
watch n ur
water vand
waterfall vandfald
waterproof vandtæt
water-ski vandski
wave n bølge
way vej
weather vejr
weather forecast vejrudsigt
week uge
weekend weekend
well godt
west vest
what hvad
wheel hjul
wheelchair kørestol
when hvornår
where hvor
which hvilken
white hvid
who hvem
whole hele
why hvorfor
wide brede
widow (female) enke; **(male)**
   enkemand
wife kone
wind vind

window vindue; **(shop)**
   butiksvindue
window seat vinduessæde
windsurfer windsurfer
wine list vinliste
wireless trådløs
wish v ønske
with med
withdraw (banking) få udbetalt
without uden
woman kvinde
wonderful vidunderlig
wood skov
wool uld
word ord
work v virke
worse værre
wound sår
write skrive
wrong forkert

X
X-ray røntgenfotografere

Y
year år
yellow gul
yes ja
yesterday i går
yet endnu
young ung
youth hostel vandrehjem

Z
zipper lynlås
zoo zoologisk have

DANISH–ENGLISH

A

adapter adapter
adgang n access; admission; entry
adresse n address
advokat lawyer
afdeling n department (shop); section; entry
afføringsmiddel laxative
afgang departure
afgangsgate departure gate
afgå depart; leave
aftale appointment
aften evening
aftryk n print (photo)
akupunktur acupuncture
alder age
aldrig never
alfabet alphabet
alkohol alcohol
allergisk allergic
allergisk reaktion allergic reaction
almindelig common (frequent); general
alt everything
altan balcony
alvorlig serious
ambassade embassy
ambulance ambulance
amerikaner American
ametyst amethyst
anbefale recommend
anbefalet registered mail
anden klasse second class
ankel ankle
ankomme arrive
ankomst arrival
anmelde report (theft)
anmodning n request

annullere cancel
ansigt face
ansigtsbehandling facial
antibiotikum antibiotic
antidepressivt middel antidepressant
antikvitet antique
antikvitetshandler antiques store
antiseptisk creme antiseptic cream
apotek pharmacy [chemist BE]
arkitekt architect
arm arm
armbånd bracelet
aromaterapi aromatherapy
astma asthma
attest certificate
Australien Australia
automatgear automatic (car)
avis newspaper
aviskiosk newsstand

B

baby baby
babymad baby food
babysitter babysitter
bad bath
badebukser swimming trunks
badedragt bathing suit
badekåbe bathrobe
badeværelse bathroom
bagage luggage [baggage BE]
bagageboks luggage locker
bagagebånd baggage claim
bagageopbevaring baggage check
bagagevogn luggage cart [trolley BE]
bageri bakery
bagerst rear

bagved behind
bakke hill
ballet ballet
bane train
bank bank (finance)
banke på knock
bar bar
barberblad razor blade
barberbørste shaving brush
barbercreme shaving cream
barbering n shave
barbermaskine razor
barbersprit aftershave lotion
bare just (only)
barn child
barnebarn grandchild
barneseng crib
barnesæde car seat; child's seat
basketballkamp basketball game
batteri battery
bedre better
begynde begin; start
behandling treatment
beholde keep
beige beige
beklager sorry
bekræfte confirm
bekræftelse confirmation
beløb n amount (money)
ben leg
benzin gas [petrol BE]
beregning per kuvert cover charge
beroligende middel tranquillizer
beskadiget damaged
besked message
beskidt dirty
beslutning decision
bestik flatware
bestille v reserve; order
bestilling n order
besøg n visit
besøgstid visiting hours
betale pay

betaling payment
betjening service (restaurant)
betyde v mean
betændelse infection; inflammation
betændt infected
bevidstløs unconscious
bh bra
bibliotek library
bikini bikini
bil car
billede photo
billet ticket
billetluge ticket office
billig cheap
bilmekaniker car mechanic
biludlejning car rental [hire BE]
biograf movie theater [cinema BE]
bjergtop n peak (mountain)
blad magazine
blandet assorted
ble diaper [nappy BE]
blegning bleach
blindtarm appendix
blist blister
blod blood
blodtryk blood pressure
blomst flower
blomsterhandler florist
blonde lace
bluse blouse
blyant pencil
blyfri unleaded (fuel)
blød soft
bløde bleed
blå blue
blåt mærke bruise
bo v live
bog book
boghandel bookstore
boksekamp boxing match
bomuld cotton
bondegård farm
bord table

borg castle
botanisk have botanical garden
brand fire
branddør fire door
brandsår burn
brandtrappe fire escape
brede wide
bremse *n* brake
brev letter
briller glasses (optical)
brite British
bro bridge
broche brooch
broderi embroidery
brug use
brug for *v* need
bruge spend
brun brown
bruser *n* shower (stall)
bryst breast
brystkasse chest
bukser pants [trousers BE]
burgerbar fast-food place
bus bus
busholdeplads bus stop
business class business class
businesscenter business center
  (at hotel)
busstation bus station
butik *n* shop
butikscenter shopping mall
  [centre BE]
butiksoversigt store directory
by town
bygge build
bygning building
byttepenge *n* change (money)
bælte belt
bære carry
bøjle hanger
bølge *n* wave
børnebassin kiddie [paddling
  BE] pool
børnelæge pediatrician

børnemenu children's menu
børneportion children's portion
børnetøj children's clothing
børste *n* brush
båd boat
bådtur boat trip
bånd ribbon

C

café cafe
campere *v* camp
camping camping
campingplads campsite
campingseng camp bed
campingvogn trailer
Canada Canada
canadier Canadian
cardigan cardigan
cd CD
centimeter centimeter
centrum downtown area [centre
  BE]
check check [cheque BE]
  (banking)
check-in skranke check-in desk
  (airport)
checkkonto checking account
chokoladeforretning candy store
cigar cigar
cigaret cigarette
cirka about
clips clip
cowboybukser jeans
creme cream (toiletry)
cykel bicycle
cykelløb cycling race
cykelsti bike route

D

dag day
dagens menu price-fixed menu
dal valley
dam pond
dame lady

Danmark Denmark
dans *n* dance
dansk Danish (language, nationality)
dansker Danish (person)
dejlig delicious
del part
delikatesseforretning delicatessen
deltage attend
deltid part-time
denim denim
deodorant deodorant
der there
desinficeringsmiddel disinfectant
dessert dessert
diabetiker diabetic
diamant diamond
diarré diarrhea
dias slide (photo)
diesel diesel
direkte direct
direktør manager
disk counter
diskotek dance club
dobbeltseng double bed
dobbeltværelse double room
dollar dollar (U.S.)
drej til turn (change direction)
dreng boy
drikkevare *n* drink
dryppe drip
dråbe drop (liquid)
dukke doll
dusin dozen
dyb deep
dyr *adj* expensive; *n* animal
dyrlæge veterinarian
dæk deck (ship)
dårlig bad
dåse can [tin BE]
dåseåbner can [tin BE] opener

E
e-billet e-ticket
e-billet check-in e-ticket check-in
efter after
efterlade *v* leave (behind)
eftermiddag afternoon
eftermiddagsforestilling matinée
efternavn surname
ekspres express
ekstra extra
elastik *n* elastic
elektricitet electricity
elektrisk electric
elektronisk electronic
elevator elevator [lift BE]
eller or
elske *v* love
e-mail e-mail
e-mail-adresse e-mail address
emalje enamel
en a (with common nouns)
en gang once
en masse lot (a lot)
en smule little (amount)
endnu yet
eng meadow
engelsk English (language)
England England
englænder English (person)
enke widow (male)
enkemand widow (female)
enkeltbillet one-way [single BE] ticket
enkeltværelse single room
entré entrance fee
et a (with neuter nouns)
et par stykker few
etage floor
etiket label
eurocheck eurocheque
Europa Europe
Europæiske Fællesskab European Union

F

fabrik factory
faktura invoice
familie family
fantastisk flot stunning
fare danger
faret vild lost
farlig dangerous
farve color
farveblyant crayon
farvel goodbye
farvning dye
fast menu set menu
fax fax
faxnummer fax number
feber fever
fejltagelse mistake
ferie vacation
fest party (social gathering)
fil file (for nails)
film movie [film BE]
filter filter
finde find
finger finger
firkantet square (shape)
fiskekort n permit (fishing)
fiskeri fishing
fjernsyn TV
flaske bottle
flaskegas butane gas
flip collar
flod river; high tide
flonel flannel
fly airplane; flight
flytte v move
fod foot
fodbold soccer [football BE]
fodboldkamp soccer [football BE] match
fodgænger pedestrian
for for
for meget too much
for varm overheated (engine)
forbindelse connection

(transportation, internet)
forbløffende amazing
forbudt forbidden
forældre parents
færdig ready
færge ferry
fødsel birth
fødselsdag birthday
født born
føle feel (physical state)
følge follow
føntørre blow-dry
før before (time)
førerhund guide dog
få motorstop breakdown (car)
få ned bring down
få pengene tilbage v refund
få udbetalt withdraw (banking)

G

gade street
gadekort street map
gaffel fork
galleri gallery
gamle bydel old town
gammel old
gang n time (recurrent occasion)
gangsti trail
garage garage
gardin curtain
gave gift; present
gavebutik gift shop
gaze gauze
gebyr n charge
gemme v save
genbrugsbutik second-hand shop
genere bother
gennem through
gennemsnitlig average
gentage v repeat
gift adj married; n poison
give give
give adgang for admitted
glad happy

glas glass; jar (container)
glemme forget
god good
godaften good evening
goddag good afternoon
godmorgen good morning
godnat good night
godt fine (OK); well
golfbane golf course
golfkølle golf club
golfturnering golf tournament
grad degree (temperature)
gram gram
grammatik grammar
gravid pregnant
gravsted tomb
grim ugly
grine laugh
gruppe group
gryde pot
grøn green
grønthandler produce store
    [greengrocer's BE]
grå gray
guide *n* guide
gul yellow
guld gold
guldsmed jeweler
gummi rubber (material)
gummisko sneaker
gynækolog gynecologist
gøre ondt hurt
gøre rent *v* clean
gå ud go out
gå væk go away
gåtur *n* walk

H

hals neck; throat
halskæde necklace
hammer hammer
handicappet disabled
handske glove
hare hare

haste urgent
hat hat
hav sea
have garden
havn harbor; port
hej hello; hi
hele whole
helgengrav shrine
helligdag holiday (public)
helsekostforretning health food
    store
hente *v* pick up (go get)
her here
herrefrisør barber
hilsen greeting
hilsner regards
himmel sky
historie history
hittegodskontor lost and found
    [lost property office BE]
hjelm helmet
hjem home
hjemmesko slipper
hjerte heart
hjerteanfald heart attack
hjertebanken palpitations
hjul wheel
hjælp assistance; help
hjælp på vejen roadside
    assistance
hjørne corner
hold team
hospital hospital
hoste *n* cough
hotel hotel
hotelfortegnelse hotel directory
hoved head
hovedpine headache
hovedpinepille aspirin
hovedtelefon headphones
hr. Mr.
hud skin
hukommelseskort memory card
hul hole

hule cave
hund dog
hurtig *adj* fast; quick
hus house
husholdningsartikel household item
hvad what
hvem who
hver each; every
hvid white
hvilken which
hvis if
hvor where
hvor langt how far
hvor længe how long
hvor mange how many
hvor meget how much
hvor som helst anywhere
hvordan how
hvorfor why
hvornår when
hygiejnebind sanitary napkin [pad BE]
hylde shelf
hyttesko loafers
hæfteklamme staple
hængekøje hammock
hæve swell
hævelse swelling
hævet swollen
høfeber hay fever
høj high; loud (volume)
høj stol highchair
højhalset turtleneck
høre på listen
hørehæmmet hearing impaired
hånd hand
håndcreme hand cream
håndklæde towel
håndlavet handmade
håndtaske purse [handbag BE]
hår hair
hårbørste hairbrush
hård hard

hårlak hairspray
hårtørrer hair dryer

I

i aften tonight
i dag today
i går yesterday
i løbet af during
i morgen tomorrow
i nærheden nearby
i stykker broken
iberegne include
id-kort identification (card)
igen again
ikke not
ikke noget nothing
ikke-ryger non-smoking
imponerende impressive
importeret imported
indbyde *v* invite
indbydelse invitation
indeholde contain
indendørs indoor
indenfor inside
indenrigs domestic (airport terminal)
indenrigsfly domestic flight
indgang entrance
indkøb shopping
indkøbscenter shopping area
indkøbsvogn cart
indløse *v* cash
indre by downtown area
indskrivning registration
indskud *n* deposit (bank)
indsprøjtning injection
indtaste *v* enter
indtil until
influenza flu
information information
informationsluge information desk
ingen none
insekt bug

insektbid insect bite
insekt-spray insect repellent
instant messenger instant messenger
interessant interesting
interesseret interested
international international (airport terminal)
internet internet
internetcafé internet cafe
investering investment
Irland Ireland
irlænder Irish
isenkræmmer hardware store
iskoldt icy (weather)

J

ja yes
jagt hunting
jakke jacket
jazz jazz
jeg I
jernbanestation train [railway BE] station
jetski jet ski
jod iodine

K

kahyt cabin (ship)
kalender calendar
kam comb
kamera camera
kamp n match (sport)
kampplads battleground
kan v can (be able to)
kapel chapel
karaffel carafe
karton carton (of cigarettes)
kasino casino
kasket cap
kasse cash desk; cashier
kasserolle saucepan
kedelig boring
kemisk toilet chemical toilet

keramik ceramics
ketsjer racket (sport)
kikkert binoculars
kilde n spring (water)
kilogram kilogram
kilometer kilometer
kilometerpenge mileage
kirke church
kirkegård cemetery
kirtel gland
kjole n dress
klage complaint
klapseng cot
klapvogn stroller [pushchair BE]
klassisk classical
klimaanlæg air conditioning
klipning haircut
klister paste (glue)
klokken o'clock
knallert moped
knap button
kniv knife
knogle bone
knæ knee
kobber copper
koble sig fra v disconnect (computer)
koble sig på v connect (computer)
kollega colleague
komme come
komme med join
komme til get (find)
komme til skade injure
komme tilbage return (give back)
kommission commission (fee)
kompas compass
koncert concert
koncertsal concert hall
konditori pastry shop
kondom condom
kone wife
konferencesal convention hall
konsulat consulate
kontaktlinse contact lens

konto account
kontor office
kontrakt contract
kontrol control
konvolut envelope
kop cup
kort card; map; *adj* short
kortspil card game
kortsynet near-sighted [short-sighted BE]
kost diet
kost broom
kramme v hug
krampe cramps
kranbil tow truck
kravlegård playpen
kredit credit
kreditkort credit card
kro inn
krone crown (Danish currency)
krop body
krus n mug (cup)
krystal crystal
kuffert suitcase
kuglepen pen
kun only
kunne able
kunst art
kunstgalleri art gallery
kunsthåndværk handicrafts
kupé compartment (train)
kurv basket
kvalitet quality
kvalme nausea
kvarter district (of town)
kvinde woman
kvindelig tjener waitress
kvittering receipt
kvæstelse injury
kysse v kiss
kæbe jaw
kæreste boyfriend; girlfriend
køb n purchase
købe buy

køje berth
køkken cuisine
køkkenchef chef
køkkenfaciliteter cooking facilities
køleskab refrigerator
kølle mallet
køn attractive; pretty
køn rute scenic route
køre drive
køre tilbage go back
kørekort driver's license
køreplan schedule [timetable BE]
kørestol wheelchair
køresyge travel sickness

L

laktoseintolerant lactose intolerant
lampe lamp
land country
landsby village
landskab landscape; scenery
lange long
langrend cross-country skiing
langsom slow
langsynet far-sighted [long-sighted BE]
langt far
lappe patch
lav low
led n joint (anatomy)
ledig vacant
ledigt free
ledigt værelse vacancy
legeplads playground
legetøj toy
legetøjsforretning toy store
leje v rent [hire BE]
lejlighed apartment [flat BE]
let light (weight)
levere deliver
levering delivery
ligeud straight ahead

liggestol deck chair
lighter lighter
lille small
lim glue
liter liter
livredder life guard (beach)
log ind login
logge af log off
logge på log on
lokal extension (phone); local
lomme pocket
lommelygte flashlight
lommetørklæde handkerchief
loppemarked flea market
lotion lotion
lufthavn airport
luftmadras air mattress
luftpost airmail
lukke v close
lunge lung
lungebetændelse pneumonia
lydguide audio guide
lygte lantern
lykke luck
lyn lightning
lynlås zipper
lys light (color)
lyserød pink
lystspil comedy
læbe lip
læbestift lipstick
læder leather
læge doctor
lægekonsultation doctor's office
   [surgery BE]
lærred linen
lår thigh

M

mad food
made v feed
madforgiftning food poisoning
madkurv picnic basket
madras mattress

maleri painting
maling n paint
manchetknap cufflink
mand husband; man
mange many
mangle v miss (lacking)
manicure manicure
mark field
marked market
marskandiser second-hand shop
massage massage
mave stomach
mavepine stomachache
med with
medbragt mad picnic
medicin medicine (drug)
meget much; very
mejeri dairy
mekaniker mechanic
mellem between
mellemmåltid snack
men but
menstruation period (menstrual)
menu menu
mere more
messe fair (event); mass (religious
   service)
meter meter
metro subway [underground BE]
metrostation subway
   [underground BE] station
middag dinner; noon
midlertidig temporary
midnat midnight
midten middle
mindesmærke memorial
mindre less
mindst at least
minut minute
miste lose
mobiltelefon cell [mobile BE] phone
mod against; toward
modtageren betaler call collect
   [reverse the charges BE]

moms sales tax [value-added tax BE]
monument monument
moppe n mop
morgen morning
morgenmad breakfast
morgenvækning wake-up call
moské mosque
motel motel
motionscenter gym
motorbåd motorboat
motorcykel motorcycle
motorvej highway [motorway BE]
mund mouth
mundvand mouthwash
mur wall
museum museum
musical musical
musik music
muskel muscle
myggenet mosquito net
mængde quantity
møbel furniture
mødelokale conference room
mødes meet
mønster pattern
mønt coin
møntvaskeri laundromat [launderette BE]
mørk dark
må may (can)
målekrus measuring cup
måleske measuring spoon
måltid meal
måne moon
måned month
måske perhaps
måtte must (have to)

N

narkose anesthetic
nat night
nationalitet nationality
naturlig natural

navn name
ned down
nedenunder below
nederdel skirt
negl nail (body)
neglefil nail file
negleklipper nail clippers
neglesalon nail salon
nej no
nem easy
nerve nerve
nogen any; anyone; someone; some
noget anything; some; something
nogle some
nok enough
nord north
normal adj normal
normalt adv usually
notesbog notebook
nu now
nummer number
ny new
nyre kidney
nær near
næse nose
næste next
nødhjælpskasse first-aid kit
nødstilfælde emergency
nødudgang emergency exit
nødvendig required
nøgle key
nøglekort key card
nål n pin (brooch); needle

O

objektiv lens (camera)
og and
også also; too
omkring around (approximately)
omkørsel detour (traffic)
område region
ondt i halsen sore throat
ondt i ørerne earache

op up
opera opera; opera house
operation operation
oplukker bottle opener
opsparingskonto savings account
optaget busy; occupied
optiker optician
opvarme v heat
opvaskemaskine dishwasher
opvaskemiddel detergent
orange orange (color)
ord word
ordbog dictionary
orkester orchestra
oval oval
ovenpå above; upstairs
overfald n attack; mugging
overfart crossing (maritime)
overfor opposite
overførsel transfer (money wire)
overskud n profit
overskæg moustache
overslag n estimate
oversætte translate
overtjener head waiter
ovn stove
oxygenbehandling oxygen treatment

P

pakke package [parcel BE]
papir paper
papirhandel stationery store
papirhåndklæde paper towel
papirslommetørklæde tissue
par pair
paraply umbrella
parfume perfume
park n park
parkering parking
parkeringskælder parking garage
parkeringsplads parking lot [car park BE]

parkeringsskive parking disc
parkometer parking meter
pas passport
pasfoto passport photo
paskontrol passport control
passe v fit
patient patient
pc computer
pedicure pedicure
pege v point
pen pen
penge money
pengeautomat ATM
penicillin penicillin
pensionat guesthouse
pensioneret retired
pensionist senior citizen
per dag per day
per person per person
per time per hour
per uge per week
perle pearl
perron platform (station)
person person
personale staff
personlig personal
petit petite
pibe pipe
pige girl
pille pill; tablet (medical)
pincet tweezers
pinkode PIN
plads seat
pladsreserveringen reservations office
planetarium planetarium
plaster n bandage [plaster BE]
plastic plastic
plasticpose plastic bag
plastikfolie plastic wrap
platin platinum
plet stain
plombe filling (tooth)
pløk peg (tent)

politi police
politianmeldelse police report
politistation police station
porcelæn porcelain
portier porter
portion portion
porto postage
post n mail [post BE]
postanvisning money order
poste restante general delivery
posthus post office
postkasse mailbox [postbox BE]
postkort postcard
pottemageri pottery
praktiserende læge doctor
  [general practitioner BE]
presse press (iron)
pris price
privat private
procentsats percentage
program program (of events)
proptrækker corkscrew
protese denture
præsentation introduction
  (social)
præsentere introduce
præventivmiddel contraceptive
prøverum fitting room
pudder powder
pude pillow
pumpe pump
pund pound (British currency,
  weight)
punktering puncture
pyjamas pajamas
pære light bulb
på on
på landet countryside
pålidelig reliable

R
rabat discount
rabatkort booklet (of tickets)
radio radio

rav amber
reb rope
recept prescription
reception reception
receptionist receptionist
redningsbælte life preserver
redningsbåd life boat
redningvest life jacket
regnemaskine calculator
regnfrakke raincoat
regning check [bill BE]
  (restaurant)
regnvejr rain
rejse journey; travel; trip
rejsebureau travel agency
rejsecheck traveler's check
  [cheque BE]
rejsefører guidebook
rejsefører travel guide
rektangulær rectangular
religion religion
ren clean; pure
rensecreme cleansing cream
renseri dry cleaner
rente interest (finance)
reparation n repair
reparere v fix; mend
reservation reservation
reserveret reserved
rest n rest
restaurant restaurant
ret dish (food item)
retsbygning court house
returbillet round-trip [return BE]
  ticket
returnere return (come back)
reumatisme rheumatism
ribben rib
ridning horseback riding
rigtigt right (correct)
ring ring (jewelry)
ringeklokke bell (electric)
rive i stykker v tear
robåd rowboat

rolig calm
romantisk romantic
roomservice room service
rubin ruby
rullegardin blind (window)
rulletrappe escalator
rumtemperatur room temperature
rund round
runde round (golf)
rundt om around (the corner)
rundtur sightseeing tour
rustfrit stål stainless steel
rute route
ryg back
ryge smoke
rygrad spine
rygsæk backpack
rød red
røntgenfotografere X-ray
røre v touch
rådhus town hall

S

safir sapphire
saks scissors
sal hall (room)
saldo balance (finance)
salg n sale
samme same
sand sand
sandal sandal
sang song
satin satin
sauna sauna
scooter scooter
se v look
seddel bill (bank note)
sejlbåd sailboat
sekund second
sele seat belt
sende send
senere later
seng bed

sent late (time)
separeret separated (relationship)
servere serve (meal)
service på værelset room service
serviet napkin
seværdighed point of interest
shampoo shampoo
side side
siden since
sidst last
sige tell
sightseeing sightseeing
sikker adj safe
sikkerhedsnål safety pin
silke silk
skaffe provide
skak chess
skakspil chess set
skarp sharp (pain)
skat tax
ske spoon
skib n ship
skilt notice (sign)
skive n slice
skjorte shirt
sko shoe
skodde shutter (window)
skoforretning shoe store
skole school
Skotland Scotland
skov forest
skovl n shovel
skrald garbage [rubbish BE]
skrive write
skrive recept på prescribe
skruetrækker screwdriver
skrædder tailor
skubbe v push
skulder shoulder
skulle have (must)
skulptur sculpture
sky cloud
skæg beard

skøjte v skate
skøjtebane skating rink
skønhedssalon beauty salon
slags sort (kind)
slagter butcher
slebet glas cut glass
slette v clear
slips tie
slipseklemme tie clip
slot palace
sluge swallow
slutning end
smal narrow
smaragd emerald
smerte ache; pain
smerter i brystet chest pain
smerter i ryggen backache
smertestillende middel
  analgesic; painkiller
sminke n make-up
smitsom contagious
smuk beautiful
snackbar snack bar
snart soon
snevejr snow
snitsår n cut (wound)
snor string
snorkeludstyr snorkeling
  equipment
sokke sock
sol sun
solbriller sunglasses
solcreme sun-tan lotion
solforbrænding sunburn
solid sturdy
solstik sunstroke
sort black
souvenir souvenir
souvenirbutik souvenir shop
sove v sleep
sovepille sleeping pill
sovepose sleeping bag
sovevogn sleeping car
spa spa

spand bucket; pail
spatel spatula
specialist specialist
specialitet speciality
spejl mirror
spil game
spillehal arcade
spillekort playing card
spise eat
spiseolie oil
spisesalen dining room
spisevogn dining car
spor track (train)
sport sport
sportsforretning sporting goods
  store
sporvogn tram
springvand fountain
sprog language
spænding voltage
spørgsmål n question
stadium stadium
stave v spell
stearinlys candle
sted n place
stegepande frying pan
stel frame (glasses)
sterlingsølv sterling silver
sti path
stige af get off
stik plug (electric)
stik n sting
stikkontakt electrical outlet
stikpille suppository
stille quiet
stilling occupation
stjerne star
stjæle steal
stof cloth; fabric; material
stol chair
stoppet blocked
stor big; large
stor størrelse plus-size
storartet great (excellent)

Storbritannien Great Britain
stormagasin department store
strand beach
strikvarer knitwear
strygejern iron (clothing)
strøm current (ocean)
strømpe stockings
strømpebukser panty hose
studere study
studerende student
studsning trim
stuepige maid
stykke piece; play (theater)
stærk strong
stævnemøde date (appointment)
støjende noisy
størrelse size
støvle boot
støvsuger vacuum cleaner
stå op get up
sulten hungry
supermarked supermarket
sut pacifier [dummy BE] (baby's)
sutteflaske baby bottle
svamp sponge
svar answer
svimmel dizzy
svimmingpool pool
svuppert plunger
svær difficult
svømme v swim
svømmebassin pool
svømning swimming
sweater sweater
sweatshirt sweatshirt
sy sew
syd south
syg ill [BE]
sygdom disease; illness
sygeforsikring health insurance
sygeplejerske nurse
symbol symbol
syn eyesight
synagoge synagogue

synge sing
synshæmmet visually impaired
syntetisk synthetic
system system
sæbe soap
sæde ved midtergangen aisle seat
sælge sell
særlig special
sæson season
sætning sentence
sætte put
sætte sig sit down
sø lake
sød sweet
sølv silver
sølvtøj silverware
så then
sår wound

T

tab loss
tage take
tage imod v accept
tage med bring; to go
  [take away BE]
tage mål af measure
tage tøjet af undress
taget taken (occupied)
tak thank you
takke thank
tale v speak
tallerken plate
tampon tampon
tand tooth
tandbørste toothbrush
tandlæge dentist
tandpasta toothpaste
tandpine toothache
tarm bowel
taske case (camera)
taske bag (purse)
taxa taxi
taxaholdeplads taxi stand [rank
  BE]

teater theater
tegnebog wallet
telefon *n* telephone
telefonbog telephone directory
telefonboks telephone booth
telefonist operator
telefonkort phone card
telefonnummer telephone number
telt tent
teltpløk tent peg
teltstang tent pole
teltunderlag groundsheet
tempel temple
temperatur temperature
tennisbane tennis court
tenniskamp tennis match
tennisketsjer tennis racket
terminal terminal
termometer thermometer
terrasse terrace
teske teaspoon
tid *n* time
tidligt early
til to
til lykke congratulations
til tiden on time
til venstre left
tilbehør accessory
tillæg *n* supplement
time hour (time)
tinlegering pewter
tjekke ud *v* check out
tjener waiter
tobak tobacco
tobakshandler tobacconist
tog train
togkort subway [underground BE] map
toilet restroom [toilet BE]
toiletartikel toiletry
toiletpapir toilet paper
told customs; duty
toldangivelsesformular customs declaration form

toldfri butik duty-free shop
toldfri varer duty-free goods
tolk interpreter
tom empty
tommelfinger thumb
torden thunder
tordenvejr thunderstorm
trafiklys traffic light
transportabel portable
trappe stairs
travlt hurry
trist gloomy
tro think (believe)
tryk pressure
træ tree
trække *v* pull
trække vejret breathe
trækul charcoal
træt tired
tråd thread
trådløs wireless
T-shirt T-shirt
tube tube
tung heavy
tunge tongue
tur tour
turistkontor tourist office
tynd thin
tyv thief
tyveri robbery
tyveri theft
tæppe blanket
tøj clothing
tøjbutik clothing store
tør dry
tørklæde scarf
tørstig thirsty
tå toe
tåge fog
tårn tower

U

uden without
udenfor outside

udenlandsk foreign
udenrigsfly international flight
udflugt excursion
udfylde fill in (form)
udgang n exit
udgift expense
udkigspost n overlook
udlejning rental
udlejningsbil rental car
udsalg sale (bargains)
udsigt view (panorama)
udskrive v print (document)
udslet rash
udsolgt out of stock; sold out
udspecificeret regning itemized
  bill
udstilling exhibition
udstillingsmontre display case
udstyr appliance; equipment
udtale pronunciation
udtryk expression
uge week
uld wool
ulykke accident
under under
underbukser underpants
underkop saucer
underlig strange
underrette notify
underskrift signature
underskrive sign
undersøgelse check-up (medical)
undertrøje undershirt
undervisning lesson
undskylde v excuse
ung young
universitet university
ur clock; watch
USA United States
uskyldig innocent

v
vaccinere vaccinate
valuta currency

vand water
vandfald waterfall
vandhane faucet
vandrehjem youth hostel
vandski waterski
vandtæt waterproof
vare article (merchandise)
varm hot; warm (temperature)
varme heat [heating BE]
vaske i hånden hand washable
vaske v wash
vaskemaskine washing machine
vaskeri laundry service
vaskerum laundry facilities
vaskesuger plunger
vasketøj laundry
ved at
ved siden af next to
vedhæng pendant
vegetar vegetarian
vej road; way
vejangivelse direction
vejkort road map
vejkryds crossroads; intersection
vejr weather
vejrudsigt weather forecast
vejskilt road sign
vekselkontor currency exchange
  office
vekselkurs exchange rate
veksle v exchange (money)
ven friend
vending phrase
vene vein
vente v expect; wait
venteværelse waiting room
ventilator fan
vest west
v-hals v-neck
vi we
vide know
videokamera video camera
vigtig important
vil gerne like

ville have want
vind wind
vindue window
vinduessæde window seat
vinhandel liquor store [off-licence BE]
vinliste wine list
violet purple
virke v work
virkelig hyggelig wonderful
virker ikke out of order
vis certain
vise vej til v direct (someone)
visitkort business card
viskelæder eraser
voldtægt n rape
volleyballkamp volleyball game
væddeløb race
væddeløbsbane race track
væk away
vække wake
vækkeur alarm clock
vælg choice
vær venlig please
værdi value
være be
værelse room (hotel)
værelsesbestillig hotel reservation
værelsesnummer room number
værktøj tool
værre worse
væske fluid
vådservietter baby wipes

W
Wales Wales
weekend weekend
windsurfer windsurfer

Z
zoologisk have zoo

Æ
ædelsten gem
ægte genuine; real
ændre v alter
ærme sleeve
æske box

Ø
øje eye
øjeblik moment
øjendråber eye drops
øjenskygge eye shadow
økonomiklasse economy class
øm sore (painful)
ønske v wish
øre ear
øredråber ear drops
ørenring earring
øst east

Å
åben open
åbne v open
år year